HOW TO ANSWER INTERVIEW QUESTIONS

Guide to a Winning Interview with Amazing Interview Answers. How to Use Emotional Intelligence to be More Confident in your Job Interview.

Jim Hunting

Table of Contents

Introduction

When attending an interview, you need to show your assertiveness, you have to practice being confident. Often, confidence starts with the mindset that you can accomplish all things on your agenda. Being more assertive starts with being proactive about your own life. When you think about what you want to do, then you can set a goal and do it faithfully. That means practicing what you preach. You have to try to do your best at what you do, because then you can be confident. It all starts with being excellent at what you do. However, even then, you can develop confidence when your skill is not the best.

Begin by getting good at what you do

One thing that you have to do is be good at what you do. That will be the first step to a successful interview process. You cannot succeed in securing a good job if you're not good at what you do. Even if you do succeed at the interview, you won't last long, if you're not skilled at the job that you want to do. Therefore, it is crucial that you find ways of developing your talent and tailoring your skills to your job. Then, you can have the qualifications necessary to get the job that you want.

Get qualified and get the education you need

The next step is getting qualified. Go and get that certificate. Get the credentials that you need to confidently submit your resume to the place where you want to work. You will need these things, because when you talk about your experience, then you can bring them up at the interview. Get as many qualifications as you can, because these will enable you to get the interview, and you'll be able to support your candidacy. The more qualified you are, the more confident you will be.

Emphasize your strong points but don't gloss over your weaknesses

Now that you are qualified, you should try to emphasize the strong points in your life that you have. Write down all your strengths on a piece of paper, and expand on each of them. Consider them deeply and think about what makes you great at what you do. Then, you can talk about your weaknesses. For every weak point that you have, try to come up with ways that you are handling these weaknesses. Think of ways you're improving yourself or finding ways to get more training and support to help you along the way. It will show some humility and the fact that you want to continually advance in your life.

Do some breathing exercises

Another thing that you should do is some deep breathing. Try to take in as much oxygen as possible before and during the interview. It is important that you are breathing a lot, because that will help you feel better. Also, if you can focus on one thing, it should be breathing in a healthy way. Try doing this, and you should notice how your nerves simply melt away.

Be positive

Believe that you deserve and are meant to be at the place where you're going to. You should show confidence, and by being positive and having a good mindset, then you'll be ready to show that you know your stuff in the interview. The important thing is to keep your chin up and keep going, even when your body is fighting and making it difficult to function while you're in the interview.

Don't fidget during the interview

Avoid making fidgety movements during the interview, which could show that you are very nervous and could make it more difficult for you. Try to remain as stationary as possible in your seat so you don't make any involuntary movements. Be conscious of your posture at all times, and keep your feet planted in front of you.

Press the pause button

Another thing that you need to do is press the pause button when you feel like you're going to veer off course. Let's say you're answering a question, and you have to talk about your previous job experience and how it was. You don't want to go off endlessly in the wrong direction about it. If you hit the pause button, then you can stop yourself from answering a question in too much detail. To answer a question succinctly and fully, you should try to say what is needed without including any additional information. Stop yourself from going any further.

Chapter 1: Before the Interview

1. Research the Backgrounds of the Interviewers*

The company you are interviewing with will typically send over the interview schedule in advance. If there are multiple rounds of interviews, you may only interview with one person the first round and then with multiple people in subsequent rounds.

It is essential to know some background details about each person who interviews you. Each interview usually begins with small talk to break the ice. Having knowledge of the interviewer's professional background goes a long way in building rapport early on. It is also an excellent way to develop relevant questions for the interviewer at the end of the session (See tip #2 for more detail).

I recommend starting your research with the company's website. If it is a small to mid-size company, you will usually come across profiles of the leadership team. Larger companies do not always publish leadership profiles. If you are unable to find the profile of your interviewer on the company's site, LinkedIn will be an excellent resource. Within each LinkedIn profile, you will find "Experience," "Skills & Endorsements," and "Activity" which will include articles or posts made by that individual to their network. There is also an "Interests" section which will show which companies and organizations that person is connected to. Reviewing the interests section is a great way to find clues about which causes and charities they focus on outside of work. I do not recommend making a "Connect" request to your interviewers on LinkedIn before the interview. They may not recognize who you are beforehand, and it is a much more natural progression to make the request after meeting them during the interview.

You can also conduct a Google search to look for articles and information on your interviewer. You will often find local news articles about business leaders getting involved in community and charitable events.

As you are conducting research on your interviewers, jot down bullet points of relevant information that you can leverage during your interview. Here is an example of what your notes might look like:

Jim Vandenberg, Director of Procurement

- Attended University of Michigan (From the dates, I'm noting that he attended when they won the 1997 national championship in football).

- Manages a team of 21 professionals responsible for sourcing raw materials, warehousing, suppliers, and logistics.
- Started career in corporate finance.
- Interested in St. Jude's Children hospital.

Possessing this background information on Jim gives you a huge advantage for the interview! The key is not to lead with any of this information but to naturally incorporate it into your conversation and leverage it to ask excellent questions. For example, you would never want to say something like:

"I saw that you were attending Michigan in 1997, did you attend any games the year the football team won the championship?"

Or

"I noted that you follow St. Jude's Hospital. What other charitable organizations interest you?"

These questions would be coming out of left field and scream to the interviewer that you investigated them. Instead, use this information during the natural progression of the conversation. For example, the interviewer will typically tell you some of their background information in the beginning. If the interview is still in the "small talk" phase and Jim stated that he attended the University of Michigan, you can say something like:

"I'm always thrilled when fall comes along and it's time for college football season. Michigan has such a rich history in football. Did they have good teams while you attended?"

You can be assured that 99 out of 100 times, Jim is going to light up like a Christmas tree and tell you about being on campus when they won the national championship. This will get him excited to discuss it with you and the interview starts out in a positive direction. If football (or whatever background information you found on the interviewer) is not your thing, do not sweat it. You certainly do not want to use the above example if you have no interest in football. However, you should be able to find something else in their background that you can relate to and bring it up when the time is right.

At the end of the interview Jim is going to ask if you have any questions. Since you researched his background information, you can ask him some excellent questions you come up with in advance such as:

"As the director of procurement, how do you take steps to mitigate the risk of large or unexpected price movements in raw materials?"

"Does XYZ Company offer employees the opportunity to get exposure working with multiple departments?"

"Does XYZ Company encourage employees to give back through charitable causes?"

Notice how each question is driven by background information from the notes above? They are also highly relevant questions that Jim will be eager to discuss.

You can certainly come to the interview with relevant questions that are not rooted in an interviewer's background information, but most candidates struggle to come up with two or three strong questions for each interviewer. Leveraging their background information is an excellent way to formulate them.

2. Develop Questions for Each Interviewer*

One of the most critical parts of the interview is towards the end when the interviewer will ask you if you have any questions for them. Not only do they expect you to ask questions, they also expect the questions to show that you did your research on the company and are genuinely excited about the position.

Candidates should be ready to ask each interviewer a minimum of 2 questions, but I always recommend having 3 questions prepared. When coming up with your questions, be sure to avoid any question that can be answered with a simple "yes" or "no" response. For example:

"Does XYZ Company offer paid leave for new fathers?"

Even though this question will probably not result in the interviewer providing a simple "yes" or "no," it is possible to be answered with a one-word response and is usually not relevant to the interview. In fact, the interviewer may not even know the answer to this question which would disrupt the flow of the conversation. This type of question should be saved for your HR contact after they offer you the job.

Your questions should be broad enough to get the interviewer thinking but specific enough to their background and role that they are enthusiastic about answering them. This is too broad of a question:

"What do employees enjoy about working at XYZ Company?"

Instead be more specific to the interviewer's role and show you did some research with this question:

"As someone who works closely with a wide range of customers in the consumer products industry, where do you look for opportunities to bring added value to your customers?"

The best way to develop highly relevant questions for each interviewer is to research their background and experience (see tip 1). Below are a couple more examples of taking notes on your research to create high quality questions.

Nicole Bennet, Accounting Manager

- Attended University of Utah, was in Beta Alpha Psi (accounting group).
- Spent time in public accounting at a Big Four Firm (PwC).
- Is responsible for overseeing quarterly and annual financial reporting with SEC and coordination of audit with independent accounting firm.
- Interested in hiking and outdoors groups.

Question 1: "What role does technology have on the challenges and opportunities facing the financial reporting profession as it relates to SEC reporting?"

Question 2: "How do you leverage student organizations on college campuses in your recruiting efforts?"

Question 3: "How does XYZ Company encourage employees to be active and participate in fitness activities?"

Kelvin Smith, Regional Sales Manager Software company

- Lives in Chicago, responsible for all Midwest sales.
- Previously was a recruiter for sales positions.
- Oversees large sales team with customers primarily in automotive manufacturing.
- Interested in Veteran Affairs and supporting VA hospitals.

Question 1: "How does your team leverage CRM (customer relationship management) technology to bring value to your customers?"

Question 2: "With software and technology changing so rapidly, how does your sales team work with the operations and technology teams to leverage customer feedback and interaction?"

Question 3: "How does XYZ Company and its employees give back to charities, veterans causes, and the local community?"

It can be challenging to remember all of your questions if you will be interviewing with multiple people. Be sure to jot them down under the name of each interviewer and bring them with you. You will typically have a brief break between interviews which will afford you the time to review them. You should usually avoid glancing down at them during the interview but just having them there will aid your confidence.

3. Ask the Interview Contact What Type of Interview to Expect

The style of the interview is dependent on the company's preference. Most companies prefer a traditional style interview where the candidate meets individually with the interviewers in separate sessions. However, some companies will conduct other types of interviews including:

*Panel interviews where multiple people observe the interview session and take turns asking the candidate questions.

*Presentation interviews where the candidate is expected to put together a presentation and present it to a group of interviewers.

*Brain teasers or test type interviews where the candidate has a fixed amount of time to complete a competency test to assess knowledge and critical thinking skills.

Some interviews are set up as a combination of the types listed above. For example, the candidate may be asked to complete a 30-minute competency test before commencing a more traditional one-on-one interview session. Regardless of the type of interview coming your way, you can be fully prepared to succeed. However, it is essential to know what type of interview to prepare for as soon as possible.

The type of interview can usually be determined by the schedule or itinerary sent over. If the company does expect you to give a presentation, they will let you know up-front. If the schedule shows you meeting with various individuals in interview sessions, you can expect to have a more traditional style interview. If your schedule only shows the beginning and end times of the interview, be sure to reach out to your contact and ask them what to expect. Being mentally prepared for one-on-one interview sessions is much different than interviewing in front of a multi-person panel. When asking what to expect, be sure not to phrase it in a way that insinuates you are looking for tips or inside information about the process. Instead, emphasize that you would like to know what to expect to help you prepare for the interview. Here is an example email you could use to send to your HR contact:

"Hi (first name),

I am looking forward to interviewing with XYZ Company on mm/dd (date). As I am starting to prepare for the interview, I wanted to reach out to you with a few questions that came up.

Should I expect the interview to be conducted in multiple sessions or will I be interviewing in front of a panel of people?

If possible, could you please provide me with the names of the people who will be included in the interview process?

Should I bring a calculator or pencils for any testing procedures?

Once again, I greatly appreciate the opportunity to interview with XYZ.

Thank you,

(your first name)

4. Take Note of the Company's "About Us" Information

Companies will almost always have a section on their website that discusses their values, culture, mission statement, history, and objectives. By absorbing this information, you will have a great sense of what they tend to look for in candidates. Many studies show that companies place a higher emphasis on cultural fit than any other trait when deciding whether to hire a candidate.

It is not uncommon for an interviewer to test a candidate on their knowledge of the company's values. They may ask the candidate which values they look for in an employer to see how well they align with the company's values. You can use the information obtained in your research to emphasize key values of your own that match up well with those of the company.

I do want to emphasize that you should not waste time memorizing everything on the company's "about us" section. It is more important to take bullet point notes of their values, mission, and culture. You can use that information to think of ways to emphasize your own values and interests that closely align with those of the company. If a company's values include the following terms:

*Integrity

*Accountability

*Diversity

*Quality

You should find ways to integrate some of these values into your answers to the interview questions. For example, if the interviewer asks you to provide them with an example of a time you faced a tight deadline on a project and in part of your answer you say, "I always place a high emphasis on quality, no matter what type of pressure I face," you have successfully aligned your answer with one of the company's values and the interviewer will usually make that connection.

5. Use Twitter/Facebook/LinkedIn to Research the Company's Personality

Social media is an excellent way to learn about the culture and atmosphere within a company. Companies will usually post news articles, press releases, updates, and engage with their audience on their social media page. Reviewing this activity on social media will give you a strong sense of their culture and tone. Is the tone they use on their social media pages very professional or is it more laid back and casual? Do they only self-promote on their pages or do they find other ways to engage with their audience? What positive news and information are they sharing with their audience?

Within a few minutes of reviewing their social media activity, you will get a strong sense of the company's culture and personality. This will usually be an indicator of the style of the interview. It may be serious and professional or more laid back and casual. You will not know for sure until the interview takes place but their activity on social media will provide a lot of clues. If any exciting updates or news articles shared by the company catch your attention, be sure to take note of them and you can bring them up during the small talk phase of the interview or even turn them into a question for the interviewer.

Chapter 2: The Power of The First Handshake

Never underestimate the power of a handshake. Handshakes are a symbol of goodwill and agreement, but it can also be used to send a strong subliminal message of authority.

There are three kinds of handshakes.

The dominant handshake that uses the palm-facing downwards to create an impression of authority. Use the dominant handshake in meetings that have a crucial agenda where the decision will either benefit or damage your firm.

While, the submissive handshake delivers the opposite message with the palm faced upward. It is never recommended to use the submissive handshake because you need to lead people and not the other way around.

And the standard handshake creates a sense of equality between two people by making both hands hold in the same manner. Make a standard handshake when you meet customers and clients to imply that you are both in the same level. This also helps make you appear approachable to people. After sealing a deal, use the standard handshake again to send a message of satisfaction.

Make your handshakes firm and warm. A firm handshake is a sign of confidence and power. In the US, women shake their hands only by holding the edge of the fingers. However, women in business don't. They still prefer the classic business shake. Holding on to the edge of the hand will make people think that their hands are dirty or you don't like them at all.

Time the handshakes well. Simply hold and pump the hands three times in an up-down motion. You can further reinforce friendship by using the other hand to slightly hold the shoulder, elbow or forearm of your partner. Finally, while you shake hands, make it sincere by brightly smiling at them. Although handshakes are a small gesture that happens only in 5 seconds, it creates positive energy both at the beginning and ending of meetings.

Establish authority with non-verbal communication

In the business world, not only do we need to create trust, we also need to build authority. Our behavior during a meeting speaks a lot about how credible and confident we are. A good show of body language can affect your sales and even job position.

Your posture and height are the one of the few things that people notice. People who are tall and stand straight are associated as being confident. This is highly important in business especially when dealing with clients. Posture creates positive energy that you are not burdened with problems. Straight posture can further add authority if your chin is slightly pointing upward and your chest is projected outward.

People get influenced easily if you speak to them while looking in their eyes. This conveys an image of seriousness and adds credibility to your message. Be mindful that you should look in a person's eyes only 60% of the time. Any more than this will intimidate your client. Use the other 40% looking at random areas beside the eye to ease tension.

While walking exude confidence and authority by swinging your arms in a firm manner. Make every action precise. Eloquence while moving make it appear that you don't make mistakes and that you calculate every movement.

Previously, we discussed the Merkel Rhombus, which is a hand gesture created by holding your hands together and forming a triangle, and then slightly moving the thumbs toward you to make a rhombus shape. The Merkel Rhombus is a new gesture that symbolizes a calm but serious behavior. Using this body language will make you approachable at the same time respected.

The Merkel Rhombus goes well with a firm and soft voice. People tend to listen more closely to a soft but audible voice rather than a loud one. A slow rhythm will make every person cling on to your every word. Just be careful not to speak too slowly because people might lose interest in you.

While standing up, take note of your feet. You might be appearing confident from the waist up, but if your legs won't lose their nerves, they'll make it obvious. Counter this by slightly opening your legs and creating a 45 degree angle between them. Refrain from moving because it might bring back your anxiety and soon you'll be shaking again.

Contrary to popular belief, putting your hands on your waist is not a sign of felinity. In fact, male executives do this gesture more than women, for you make it appear that you are calm and relaxed in the face of stressful activities.

Combining these non-verbal authoritative cues to gestures that establish rapport will help you become an effective businessman. Non-verbal communication greatly increases your charisma that persuades people to agree to you.

Chapter 3: Questions About Your History

After they get a good sense of who you are inherently, they are going to start to pull information from you to determine what experience you have. If you are a good person with a good head on your shoulders and have a good sense of responsibility, then of course, you've already passed the first part of the interview. The thing is, just being a good person doesn't mean you are always the right candidate for the job.

These types of questions will help them to see your history, what kind of educational experiences that you have, and what skills and lessons from your last job you will bring into this one. These are questions that will give the person conducting the interview the greatest sense of the type of employee that you would be.

"Why did you leave your last position?"

Now this is the juicy part, where you start to reveal all the reasons that you are here. The employer is asking you this because they want to know why things didn't work out. Was the other position just not right for you?

Did you leave your last job for a similar reason that you might end up leaving this job at this company you are trying to work at? They're going to want to know what happened to get a better insight into what went on. Spare them the dramatic details and keep it professional.

"I left my last position because I felt as though there was no room for advancement. I lacked creative control and I felt that my voice wasn't being heard. I needed a positive change in my life because I want to continue to grow and move forward."

"How did you find out about this current position?"

The reason that employers might want to know this is because it will reveal even more about you. First, they are going to want to know if you know anyone that already works there. This gives them a personal recommendation which can be helpful in understanding who you are. They are also going to want to know if you were actively job-hunting and being proactive about finding a new position, or if this is just something that slipped into your lap. They are also going to be interested in figuring out if any of their marketing tactics to reach out to other potential candidates are working or not.

"I actually found a listing for this job on an online job board. I have been looking and applying to several places and the objectives and job description of this position intrigued me."

"Can you tell me about a time where you went above and beyond and did even more than what you were expected to do?"

This is a hard question because it will put you on the spot. Employers still want to see if you can come up with information like this quickly and without another prompt. Though challenging, you will still want to have a specific example so that they can truly see the nature of your character. You will want to pull preferably from a time period when you were working somewhere else. Don't lie and make yourself sound extra good – they will be able to tell. Be honest and speak from experience because it will be easier to remember this event when it comes time to talk about it then. Describe not just how you were able to go beyond what you were asked to do, but how you also managed to help the business out in some way as well. This would be a good answer, but remember to keep it specific to the scenario and not to base it verbatim of ours:

"There was a time when I used to work at the ice cream store in my hometown. At night, it would be our duty to clean the place up and then clock out. The morning staff would be responsible for setting up for the next day. One night we were rather slow, so I decided to do all of the morning prep. The next day, the workers came in and didn't have to do much at all, making their morning start off easier. On top of that, they were able to open early and let some people in the store who had already been waiting."

"How would your last boss, manager, or supervisor describe you as an employee?"

This is another great question that they will likely ask you in some form or other. They want to know not just what you are like as an employee, but as someone who takes orders from the higher-ups. Were you feared by them? Did they have trouble telling you things? Were they your best friend? This previous relationship with the higher-ups will be important in helping them see what benefits you might bring to the position as an employee.

"I would say that I had a pretty good relationship with my last supervisor. We had open communication and instead of her always telling me what to do, we worked together to delegate tasks that I was better at to me and delegate tasks that she was better at to her, always checking in with each other to make sure both of our needs were being met."

"Can you describe to me a time in the past at a different position in which you were faced with a very challenging scenario, and what you did in the moment to resolve the issue?"

This is a good question where your answer will show that you are recognizing what you might have struggled with in the past, and how you handle pressure when you are faced with an obstacle. Remember to stay honest, and don't feel the need to go into every last agonizing detail about this.

"There was a time when I worked retail at a small gift shop. I noticed that a woman was stuffing some smaller jewelry pieces into her purse. She was standing right by the door, so I feared that she was going to make a run for it. I asked her if she needed any help and showed her some merchandise at the back of the store to buy me time while I talked to the owner. She was about to leave when I asked her if she was going to pay for the items in her purse. After retrieving the items, the owner and I decided to let her go since it was less than $30 worth of merchandise, but we made sure she wasn't allowed back in. I panicked at first and wanted to stop her immediately, but that could have turned into a messy situation, so I tried to remain as calm as possible and work with my supervisor to find the right solution."

"What is something that you saw a different employee do that you wouldn't do yourself? Can you describe a time when a coworker did something they shouldn't do? How did you handle this?"

This question might be phrased in a few different ways, but it's an important one that will give them insight into what you believe a good employee should be like. There are a ton of employees who do the wrong thing, so when you can show that you recognize the difference between right and wrong, it makes you all the more trustworthy. Don't shame anyone, don't use names, and make sure that you aren't being rude. Simply state what they did wrong, why it was wrong, and how you would have corrected the situation. Here is an example:

"There was a time in my last job when my coworker would always leave her leftover tasks for the person that came into the next shift. Even though she worked a slower shift, there would still be leftover tasks that she didn't bother to complete. Initially, I confronted her about it. I made sure all my tasks were done and left a note asking to help out during the slow shifts since ours were busier at night. She ended up ignoring this, so I had a discussion with my boss, and we came up with the perfect task list that fairly delegated the right amount of duties."

"What was the best part about your last position?"

This is a question that will let your interviewer know what you value the most in the workplace. When you can discuss with them the benefits of a position, they will be more likely to see what things you are passionate about. Be honest with this, but of course keep it professional. You might have enjoyed that you had a few hours a day to sit on your phone after the boss went home, or maybe you liked that you got a free meal every shift. Keep it professional. Say something like this:

"One of the best parts of my last job was the sense of community that was there. Everyone got along and we all managed to work together in a harmonious way, playing off each other's strengths and weaknesses. It was unfortunate when I had to leave, but luckily, I still keep in contact with many of the same people and have no issue including them in my life to this day."

"If you were in a position where you had to fire someone, how would you do it? Have you ever had to let someone go in the past? What is your method for doing so?"

Not every position that you are interviewing for is going to require you to have to fire someone. There might still come a time when you have to be a part of the process of letting someone go. This is a challenging scenario that requires someone empathy, but also strong enough to reveal the truth. Even if you don't think you'd ever be in that position for the job that you are interviewing for, it's still important to have an answer to this question. Start by saying something such as this:

"I never have had to do this in the past, but I would imagine it would be a difficult scenario. If I ever had to, I would start by ensuring that I am in a private room with the person so as not to embarrass them. I would let them know the reason there is an issue in the first place, and then gently reveal to them what is going to happen next. I'd give them the remainder of the day to clear out if they wanted to but give them the freedom to decide when to leave during the day."

"What has been your greatest achievement in life? What about in your career?"

This question is usually asked because they want to know what your biggest accomplishment is. Think about what has been the single most important time in your life or something that you are proud of to share with others. They want to see your passion as you talk and find out how you might have been able to improve your own life.

Make sure that when you share this you give a personal or a career related answer, depending on how they might end up asking.

"My greatest achievement was certainly getting my Master's degree. Before I even applied to graduate school, I was nervous. I thought I wouldn't be able to do well because I had a bad semester as an undergrad. I let this become my source of motivation and graduated at the top of my class! Whenever I doubt myself I don't use my degree as a reminder, but instead, my dedication that was required for all the hours of studying and homework to remind me of all the things that I'm capable of."

Chapter 4: Talking About Your Advantages And Disadvantages

"Tell us about your pros and cons" - this is probably one of the most common questions in the interview. Someone is offered to name three of their weaknesses and three strengths, others are asked to describe the personality traits that hinder or help them in building a career – there are a plenty of options how recruiters formulate this question.

First, let's understand why this issue consistently ranks among the most frequently asked during the interview. What recruiters want to hear from the candidates? Honest confession of laziness and lack of organization or pompous speech of "I have virtually no weaknesses"?

Neither one nor the other. By asking the applicant about his advantages and disadvantages, a specialist of recruitment wants to know how mature is a person sitting in front of him, what is his self-esteem, if he is able to work constructively, including on himself. as it is known, there are no people without flaws: we are all woven of good and bad qualities. Namely in their recognition psychologists tend to see a sign of a stable and mature personality.

However, you do not need to invent anything to show recruiters that you fully meet the job requirements. Lying at the interview will not help you make a career. Be honest, but think over your answer in view of the given recommendations:

Lows in the pros. Psychologists believe that the best practice is response to a question about the shortcomings at the interview indirectly pointing out own advantages. "Friends think I'm meticulous. I really scrupulous, like checking all the details, and it annoys people. But I'm trying to learn to look at things more widely," – this is an excellent response of the applicant applying for the position of design engineer. "I think I am over-talkative, perhaps this is a consequence of my profession" - a good option for a candidate for the position of PR-manager or marketing specialist.

Another option of answer to the question about the shortcomings is to mention the lack of professional knowledge, not directly related to the desired position. Thus, you will demonstrate your recruiters frankness and willingness to develop. For example, if you are applying for a position of news feed reporter, you can safely admit that so far have not mastered the genre of the essay: in this work, you likely will not need this skill in the near future. However, you should still be careful not to harm yourself - think carefully about the answer.

Think about how the qualities which you are going to tell recruiters will create for you a competitive advantage over other candidates. For example, do not point to your leadership skills where they are not needed. "I'm pretty ambitious," - says the candidate for the post of accountant in a company with an established structure and ... left without a job offer. But in the young company, vigorously seizing market, such quality may well come in handy.

How to answer personal questions during the interview? In preparation for the interview, many job seekers think through in advance the answers to possible questions - about the professional accomplishments, the reasons for leaving previous job, career goals. But personal questions are often taken by surprise. What recruiters want to know, asking, for example, about the reasons for divorce or the presence of chronic diseases in the child? How to respond to such questions, and whether to do it?

In most cases, questions about the private life are not caused by idle curiosity of recruiters; they have very specific goal - a more or less accurate psychological profile of the candidate. Experienced hiring managers know that often information which, at first glance, is not related to the professional qualities of the applicant, says more about him than he was talking about himself. That is why many HRs go for a violation of ethical norms and show interest to the private life of the candidate.

For the successful employment psychologists advise not to neglect the possible answers to personal questions: "What you care about that?" "Why do you want to know?" - such counter-questions to address HR management hardly will benefit your career. Try to find an opportunity to respond, and if the question seems too personal, politely and gently turn the conversation in another direction.

"Do you live with parents or separately?" - it would seem, what does this have to do with future work in the position of sales manager? Meanwhile, detailed response to this question can talk about such personal characteristics of the applicant, as the maturity, independence, responsibility towards the family, as well as on the level of his income. If a candidate talks about high earnings in the previous place of work, but he lives in a studio apartment with his parents or other relatives, recruiter may begin to doubt his sincerity, and hence the level of professionalism.

"Do you have your own apartment or rent it?" – this is another frequent question during the interview. At first glance, what interest business recruiter has to jobseekers property? Most likely, in such way the personnel manager is trying to understand the structure of your costs. It's one thing if the candidate has his own housing, the other - if he is forced to save each month rather big amount to pay the rent of apartment, and the third - if he pays the mortgage. In addition, the answer to this question will help supplement your psychological portrait of valuable information - whether you are willing to bear a serious responsibility to the credit institution.

Many young women have heard on interview questions like, "When you are planning to have a baby?" Of course, this is a very personal question, and often job applicant lost in answering it. After all, it is not always possible to accurately plan the birth of a baby: it is a question not only of the desire but also the state of health.

Desire of recruiter to know about your plans is clear: not all employers are willing to invest in the adaptation of the employee, which soon plans to leave on maternity leave. How to answer this question - directly or evasive, you decide. "In the near future we do not plan to have children" – such a response do not oblige you to anything, and thus dispels some fears of employer.

By law, you cannot be refused to be accepted for a job if you want to become a mother, or are already pregnant. However, it is likely that the true cause of refusal in this case will not be communicated.

"How often your child is sick?" is one more personal question, often asked by women during the interview. At this, for recruiter it does not matter what the temperature accompanies a cold in a baby - he is more concerned about the frequency and duration of your sick lists. It is better to answer frankly, because it is important also for you: the HR manager asks you to prioritize. If the career for you at the moment is no less important than the education of offspring, boldly answer that there is someone to look after baby. "The child is sick as often as other children, but grandmother (nurse, husband, etc...) is ready to stay with him" - this answer is quite satisfactory for the employer.

"What are you fond of?", "Do you have any hobbies?" – asking such questions recruiters are trying to figure out what are your temperament and character, whether you are suitable for the position by personal qualities. If, for example, the candidate claims to PR-manager position in a young and rapidly growing company, but says that he spends weekends in a chair knitting, the manager on staff will have reasonable doubts in his sociability.

"What is the last book you read?" – this is a question for revealing the overall development of the candidate. What he reads - only professional literature or finds the time to reread the classics? Although the objectivity of this method could be argued, it is still applied. There is no need to compose a list of literature, which, as it seems to you, makes you smarter in the eyes of a hiring manager. It is better to call the two books that you really have read recently: one professional and one fiction. Thus, you show that you develop not only as a professional but also as a person.

Personal questions are not uncommon in the interviews, and how you respond to them, to some extent, the decision about accepting you in a new team depends on. Therefore, talking with recruiters, be polite, diplomatic and sincere. If you do not want to respond to some particularly personal question - calmly and kindly tell that you are not ready to discuss it.

Chapter 5: Power Words to Blow Them Out Of The Water

Your goal in an interview is to make an impression and stand out from the crowd. There are some words that you can use to do just that. Barry Drexler, an interview coach, has conducted more than 10,000 interviews, and with his experience in HR, he has come up with 12 of the most powerful words that you should use in the interview process.

Leadership and management

You may not be applying for a position as a manager, but many companies want to know that you have some experience in this area, because you may be called upon to lead a team or give orders in some capacity. Even Burger King has some supervisors. So, if you can say things like "I managed a team of workers or I led a group of colleagues," then you can have a leg up in the process, because you demonstrate that you have skills that can eventually lead to leadership opportunities, even within this company.

Strategy and plan

Employers view candidates who have a strategic plan in mind more favorably. If you have experience with roles or responsibilities that required strategy, it shows that you have a background that is necessary to take on challenges and difficulties that may come your way in your new role. If you have a plan, then you know what to do and what steps you need to take to achieve the goals and complete tasks that are required for the job function. It also shows that you are a visionary who will carry out a plan to completion.

Established

Drexler says this word is powerful, because it shows that you have been able to complete a project and it demonstrates your authorship of a strategy or plan that was carried out. For example, you could say that you established a certain plan for a company. That would carry a lot of weight, because you authored the plan that was completed and accomplished a goal for the company.

Results and achieved

Employers love it when you talk about what you have achieved. This shows that you were able to reach the objectives that you had set. It also shows that you are a committed employee who always follows through on promises, goals, and other objectives that are set. It also gives you a sense of credibility and proves you are trustworthy as a worker. It is powerful for the interviewer to hear about the goals you have achieved.

Influence

Another word that is important is influence. When you show that you have influenced others, then you show yourself to be both a reliable and interesting candidate. You can talk about how you influenced the management to carry out some kind of plan. Instead of saying, "My managers really liked my plan," you could say, "I influenced the management to carry out this action plan, which succeeded in growing the business."

Recommend and suggest

When you use these words, you show that you are willing to contribute to the growth of the organization and want to do your best to promote your own plans and persuade the management to follow your advice and ideas. For example, you could say, "I recommended that my boss do _____, and they listened to my

counsel. In the end, the business succeeded in
_____."

Collaborate

When you use the word "collaborate", you indicate that you can work well with others. You're not just working for yourself. Instead, you're proving that you can be a member of a team and contribute meaningfully to it. You can talk about how you collaborated with others and how you were a key member of a group. You could say something like, "I collaborated with the marketing team to produce a strategy that worked for the company."

Example

Isaac is in an interview to get the position of data analyst.

Isaac: As you can see on my resume, I collaborated with many members of the data analysis team at my previous job. We were able to accomplish numerous tasks which enabled the company to move forward.

Interviewer: Isaac, would you tell us about a time where you had to lead a team?

Isaac: Yes, in fact, I led a team last year. We analyzed a survey that had been carried out by Coca Cola, and we were able to accomplish a goal. I collaborated with the members of the team. We succeeded in _____. In addition, I recommended to my manager that we do _____. In the end, my recommendation helped the organization to achieve the aim of _____.

Isaac used several keywords that were powerful and would wield influence over the decision of the HR team. He used to "accomplish", "collaborate", "succeed", "achieve", and "recommend", all of which would be helpful in securing him the position on the team.

Conclusion

It is important that you find ways that you can become more confident during an interview. You can use some power words to get you going. Always remember to be positive and reflect on your past experience, emphasizing what you were able to take from each aspect of your background. Strengthen your case by talking about your accomplishments, how you overcame adversity, and the skills that you can bring to the position. The main thing is matching your skills and experience with the position and proving why you would be the best candidate for the job. You have to find persuasive ways to do that. It all starts with your language and the words you choose to project your image. Remember that you have all the background and skills necessary to do it. All you need to do now is to communicate it and make your case. Then, you can achieve your goal and snag your dream job!

Chapter 6: People Skills Questions

Employers don't just care if you can do the job—lots of people can. What they want to know is if you want to do the job (your motivation) and if you'll fit in with the rest of the people you need to deal with (your people skills) on the job.

For this reason, behavioral interviewing is very common, which means the interviewer will ask lots of nosy questions about your past behavior, believing there's no better way to predict your future actions than by hearing about your previous actions in similar situations. You may also encounter situational interviewing, in which you are asked hypothetical questions so the interviewer can see how you react in imaginary situations, which may or may not take place in this job.

Behavioral interviewing asks lots of questions about your past behavior, because of the belief that past actions are the best predictors of your future actions in similar situations. Situational interviewing poses hypothetical questions like "what if or "let's say" to see how you'd behave in possible situations.

What is your management style? Or: Give me an example of when you had to show good leadership. Or: Describe your leadership style or skills...

What the interviewer is asking/looking for: In most industries, the ability to manage people is considered important to advancement in your career. Because of this, the interviewer wants to know how you lead, plan, organize, and control things—the four main components of management.

Good answer: Think about times when you got things done with the help of other people—if not at work, then in your volunteer, leisure, or school activities. Then think about good bosses and bad bosses you've had and why they were good or bad. Perhaps your bad boss used to give you deadlines and then ask a week before the due date where the project was, or yell at you without explaining what you did wrong, or hog all the credit.

You learned by negative example that a good boss gives credit where it is due, communicates clearly, and is fair. In addition, criticism of your work should be constructive, pointing out what you did wrong and what you need to do to improve without attacking you personally. Your answer should reflect some of these good traits, and be ready to give an example or two from your experience.

Bad answer: Anything that shows you haven't managed people at all or thought about how you deal with them. Or that you display the hallmarks of a bad boss.

How do you motivate people you manage?

What the interviewer is asking/looking for: He or she wants to see you are generous with praise and credit for a job well done, and possess enough insight to know different people are motivated by different things, instead of following a cookie-cutter management approach.

Good answer: Show that you aim to inspire and teach the people you manage and respect their individual differences, instead of being an autocrat who issues orders with no explanation.

Bad answer: An answer that reveals you don't bother much about motivating your underlings—and as far as trying to understand their differences, forget it.

Tell me about your track record for promoting your staff...

I had a team of 12 sales people and 8 of them got promoted in the last two years.

What the interviewer is asking/looking for: The interviewer wants to know you have the "right stuff" in terms of identifying talented workers and helping develop their potential so they can contribute to the best of their ability to your organization.

Good answer: Having staffers who rise in your organization reflects well on you as a manager, so hopefully your success ratio in this area is good and you can give an example or two to prove it.

Bad answer: An answer that shows you never met an underling you liked enough to develop them, which does not reflect well on your skills as a manager.

5 years ago (as an assistant) he really wanted to leave the company but I managed to convince him not to do so – and now he is the operations manager.

What the interviewer is asking/looking for: He or she wants to see that you can spot talent and potential, and point out a flaw that can stand some improvement tactfully, without losing the employee.

Did you watch The Apprentice, the hit TV reality show where job-hunters compete for a top, well-paying spot in Donald Trump's company? Well, lessons from the series are being taught at top business schools nationwide, as MBA students study how the job-seekers learned to think on their feet, take risks, choose their team, and defend their actions. Some major lessons from The Apprentice include:

• Bosses want to hire people who are like others on their current team.

• Pay attention to what the boss says are his or her company values.

• You're always being interviewed.

• You have to fight to get the job.

• Show respect for your peers.

• All companies want team players who pitch in.

Good answer: Give an example that shows how you were able to smooth a diamond in the rough's edges, or clarify how to produce good results in your organization, to enable the employee to reach his or her potential.

Bad answer: An answer that shows you are not skilled at people-problem solving, and don't really know how to salvage a talented employee with a flaw or two.

Describe a time when a personal commitment interfered with a business crisis or last-minute meeting...

I had a last-minute meeting with the CEO and the same afternoon my son had a very important soccer game, so I asked my wife to record it with our camcorder. The next day me and my son watched the entire game at home (eating popcorn, hot-dog, things like that) and it was fun!

What the interviewer is asking/looking for: He or she wants to know if, when the going gets tough, you'll be running off to a personal appointment, or you can be counted on when your employer really needs you.

Good answer: Give an example of how you rescheduled your personal commitment, or arranged to have someone else handle it, to show how loyal you are when your employer is in a crunch.

Bad answer: A remark or nonverbal cue that shows resentment and/or incredulity that your employer may ever expect to come above your personal life in your list of priorities.

How did you get along with your last work team?

I worked well with my team and their different personalities.

What the interviewer is asking/looking for: Trust me, the interviewer does not want to hear the gory details about the ghastly coworkers you are forced to put up with, any more than hearing about your boss, the head ogre.

Good answer: Give an example of how the team pulled together to achieve a goal. Show that you are cooperative and pleasant as well as a good worker.

Bad answer: A litany of how lazy, incompetent, or mean-spirited your team members were, in contrast to you, a saint.

Lace your answers with "we" and "our," not just "I," to signify you are a team player who has the employer's interests at heart, not just your own.

Can you give an example of how you increased sales, saved money, saved time, or improved efficiency at your job?

I handled my workload more efficiently by holding calls and returning them at a certain time of day to give me uninterrupted working time.

What the interviewer is asking/looking for: These are an employer's major goals, so the interviewer wants to know if you've ever brought "added value" by making a meaningful contribution in any of these crucial areas.

Good answer: Tell the interviewer about any time you brought in new business or made a suggestion your employer acted on—a potential client to pitch, an advertising or publicity campaign you dreamed up that increased a client sales and led to more business with your firm, an employee you referred, researching a cheaper way to deliver a product you worked on.

Bad answer: You can't think of any time you demonstrated "added value" to your employer. Isn't it enough you come in 9 to 5 five days a week?

Substance versus style: Most employers want both. They want to know you can do the job well (substance) as well as act appropriately with people you have to deal with (style).

What would you describe as a good work environment?

It is where talent and hard work are recognized and rewarded.

What the interviewer is asking/looking for: He or she wants to feel a work atmosphere you can thrive in mirrors their own, and is eager to avoid a bad fit like a very laid-back person in a pressure-cooker environment, which you will feel impelled to quit at the first opportunity.

Good answer: If you have any idea from your research what the work environment is like at this employer, try to reflect it in your answer. If not, say something like an atmosphere where people are motivated to pull together to produce a quality product or service. Who can argue with you?

Bad answer: An environment that bears no resemblance whatsoever to the employer in question, which means your days there will probably be numbered or you will do your work perpetually disgruntled.

Constructive criticism points out what you did wrong and what you need to do to improve without attacking you personally (for example, by berating you as stupid or incompetent).

How do you handle rejection?

I don't take rejection personally, but as an abstract turn-down of a product or service I am representing.

What the interviewer is asking/looking for: Because rejection is a crucial part of any job in sales, which includes public relations, customer service, and telemarketing, the interviewer wants to make sure you are secure enough to bounce back after being rejected, instead of taking it personally and feeling miserable.

Good answer: Rejection often gives you helpful information about how to convince your next sales prospect or overcome the objection of your current prospect, thus increasing your success ratio.

Bad answer: Any clue that you are insecure and will act devastated, defensive, or nasty after rejection, which will interfere with doing your job well.

How would your coworkers describe you? Or: How would your supervisor describe you?

Enthusiasm, reliability, integrity, and being a team player.

What the interviewer is asking/looking for: This is a cagey way for the interviewer to find out what you're really like at work, in the words of coworkers and bosses.

Good answer: Hopefully they will have recognized some of your greatest strengths. Cite some strengths employers tend to admire.

Bad answer: Blurting out how coworkers and your supervisor see you unfairly, and how they are wrong.

How far do you want to rise (or see yourself rising) in our organization?

As far as my skills and the employer will allow.

What the interviewer is asking/looking for: He or she wants to gauge your level of ambition and future orientation. Giving them a sense of how motivated and goal-directed you are is more important than naming a specific job title.

Good answer: Obviously, your advancement will hinge both on your doing well and your accomplishments being recognized and rewarded by the employer, so try something noncommittal. If your goal is to head the department you would be joining, or become sales manager for a larger territory, say so.

Bad answer: Anything that shows you have given no thought to your future beyond the job you are applying for. On the other hand, saying "I want your job" generally is a bit too bold for most interviewers.

Summary

"People skills" are important, and by now the interviewer has a pretty good sense of how you get along with people, manage people, and cope with people when they're difficult.

You've now described your style with examples of how you've acted in the past, while he or she already knows your substance or qualifications. He or she also has a sense of what you think is a good work environment, if you've ever brought added value by increasing sales or saving money (which is dear to any employer's heart), as well as how far you want to go.

• Be prepared to give examples of how you handled past situations at work.

• Be prepared to describe how you are a team player who gets along with many different types of people.

• Be prepared to give examples of how you increased sales, saved money or time, or increased efficiency at work.

• You may be asked how you would handle hypothetical situations at work.

Chapter 7: Industry Related Questions

Tell me about a time when you went above and beyond expectations for a project or assignment.

Question Type:

Behavioral

Question Analysis:

One of the most common performance ratings for a hardworking and competent employee is "meets expectations" however, there will be opportunities when an employee should think outside of the box and go above and beyond the call of duty. Interviewers want to know that the candidate is willing to embrace these opportunities instead of shying away from them. You should discuss an example of a time when you identified an opportunity to exceed expectations and took advantage of it to bring value to your team or to a customer.

What to Avoid:

You should avoid opportunistic dialogue such as "I always exceed expectations." The interviewer will know this is not a realistic response. You should avoid examples that would be expected of any normal hardworking employee such as "I had a tight deadline coming up, so I worked 50 hours one week instead of my normal 40."

Example Response:

S/T: In my previous position as a web developer, I was assigned to a project to help a new customer integrate a payment processor for their ecommerce platform. As I was reviewing their website code, I noticed some unrelated HTML errors that were hurting their search engine optimization. I estimated that it would take me an extra twelve hours to fix the code, but I had no extra time in my schedule.

A: I explained the situation to my manager and asked for permission to do the work for the customer outside of my current work commitments. She was impressed that I took the initiative to bring additional value to a new customer at the expense of my evenings over the next week. I informed the customer about the errors and explained the SEO value it would bring if I corrected them.

R: Both my manager and our customer were appreciative that I was willing to work the extra hours at no additional charge to correct the issue for them. They ended up choosing our firm for a major project three months later and mentioned their earlier experience working with me as a deciding factor.

Tell me about a time you had to meet a tight deadline. What was the outcome?

Question Type:

Behavioral

Question Analysis:

The interviewer will ask this question to assess how well the candidate works under pressure and to see if they are willing to go the extra mile. You should provide an example of an unexpected situation that involved careful planning and required you to go above and beyond normal expectations.

What to Avoid:

You should avoid providing an example that is associated with a routine task such as "our monthly report was due the next day, but I had not started it yet" because you likely would have known about the deadline in advance, so it can appear as though it is only a tight deadline due to poor planning. Unless there was a significant unforeseen circumstance, you should also avoid discussing an example of a tight deadline which you or your team were not able to meet it.

Example Response:

S: In my previous role as a systems analyst, I lead a project to implement an EDI integration for a client's new procurement software.

T: Two weeks before the project deadline, the client informed us of a significant issue with their legacy software which was having a major impact on their day-to-day business. They asked if we could accelerate our timeline to deliver our project in five days. My manager and I discussed the situation and agreed to let the client know we would do everything we could to meet their new request.

A: I brought our team together to explain the situation and let them know that we would be focusing our time exclusively on this project to try to meet the accelerated deadline. I mapped out all remaining tasks on a whiteboard and we agreed on completion dates for each task over the next five days. I also scheduled daily update meetings to ensure we were staying on track and available to each other when issues came up.

T: We worked 14 hours per day over the next five days but through our collaboration and perseverance we completed the project on time. The client was extremely happy with results of the project and our manager gave each of us three extra vacation days for our hard work.

Tell me about a time you disagreed with your boss. How did you handle it?

Question Type:

Behavioral

Question Analysis:

The interviewer will use this question to assess how well the candidate handles a disagreement with someone in an authoritative position. The response will say a lot about the type of working relationship the candidate might have with a future boss. Your example should show that you have confidence in speaking candidly with your boss while still respecting their point of view and authority. You should try to think of a situation in which you disagreed with a situation but offered an alternative solution.

What to Avoid:

In your example, you should avoid personally criticizing your boss. This can raise a warning flag about your character. You should also avoid examples in which you raised the disagreement with your boss in the presence of other team members. Unless your boss encouraged feedback in a group setting, disagreements with those in authority should be handled in a one-on-one setting.

Example Response:

S: In a prior role as a procurement analyst, I was on a team that worked on procurement process efficiency through the measurement of purchasing history and inventory turnover trends. In an effort to add more reporting functionality to our purchasing history, our boss worked on a project to switch us over to a new software package.

T: Although the reporting functionality had improved, the new software did not integrate directly with our company's ERP system, so we were required to manually upload our purchase history which often took us hours to do.

A: I set up a meeting with my boss to explain my experience and concerns with the software. I first told him that I appreciated his hard work in seeking to find better reporting solutions. I then explained that I felt the benefits of the new software were outweighed by the time it took our team to manually add the purchasing history data which slowed down our analysis. As an alternative solution, I showed him documentation of research I had done on comparable software that could be integrated with our ERP system.

R: My boss was appreciative of me being upfront and honest about the change. He also thanked me for my research on the software solution I came up with and one month later we ended up switching over to it.

What do you like most about working in this industry?

Question Type:

Industry and Company Specific

Question Analysis:

The interviewer will ask this question for a couple reasons. First, a new hire is an investment for the company, so they want to validate the candidate's passion and long-term commitment to the industry. They will also use the question to see how well the response aligns with the duties of the job. When discussing your favorite aspects about the industry, be sure to highlight those that are highly relevant to the position.

What to Avoid:

You should avoid discussing characteristics that do not pertain to the position. For example, if you are interviewing for a marketing position and the job description desires competency in Adobe Photoshop, you would not want to express how much you love working with Affinity Photo (Mac competitor to Photoshop). You should also try not to be too vague in your response. "I love that I get to work with people" does not sound nearly as good as "I enjoy working directly with clients to diagnose their challenges and offer solutions that bring them a better return on investment on their advertising budgets."

Example Response:

The thing I enjoy most about offering software solutions in the sales industry is that no two days are ever the same. I have the opportunity to work with such a wide range of clients who possess diverse challenges and needs for their human resource systems. I take pleasure in fostering client relationships. To me, success looks like a client reaching out for help with confidence that I can solve their problem. Believe it or not, I also really enjoy the travel associated with this industry. I consider it an opportunity to be able to explore new cities while I am traveling to meet with current and prospective clients.

What was the most difficult decision you have made in the past year?

Question Type:

Behavioral

Question Analysis:

Candidates without management experience will often get tripped up over this question because they have not had to make what would traditionally be considered a difficult decision such as cutting a budget or laying off an employee. However, there are plenty of opportunities to discuss difficult decisions outside of management roles. The interviewer is looking for an answer that demonstrates rationale and strong problem-solving skills. You should discuss an example that shows your ability to weigh options and critically think through the situation before coming to the decision. Some examples of tough decisions include: reporting unethical behavior, providing a negative review for a co-worker, choosing a new vendor, and turning down a promotion.

What to Avoid:

You should avoid discussing personal decisions that are not relevant to the position such as "I decided to purchase my first home last year" or "three months ago, I decided it was time to break it off with my fiancé." The interviewer is looking for your decision-making capabilities in a professional setting. Your answer should include the result of your decision, so you should avoid examples where the decision lead to an unfavorable outcome.

Example Response:

S/T: In a previous role selling professional services for IT projects, I was offered a promotion to be our company's Midwest resource services manager. I was honored to be offered the promotion and asked my boss for a few days to consider it. The new position would have increased my responsibilities while offering a raise in pay. At the time, I was in critical stages of a few projects with my clients. I was also making inroads with prospective clients that would soon lead to new business. Before the promotion came up, I had a strong interest in exploring future opportunities within the company's marketing team which would be a change to a new department.

A: I set up a meeting with my boss to discuss my desire to remain in my current position as well as my inclination to find an opportunity in the marketing department for my next career move.

R: At first, he was a little surprised that I decided to turn down the promotion, but he agreed with me that I brought the most value to our clients by remaining in my current position. He thanked me for my honest assessment and connected me with a manager in the marketing department to discuss future opportunities.

What motivates you?

Question Type:

Ambition

Question Analysis:

Candidates often struggle with this question because it is so broad in nature. The interviewer is typically using the question to understand what type of work is encouraging and fulfilling to the candidate. Coming up with an answer does require some personal reflection but ultimately your response should be centered around positive results or characteristics in the professional setting. Ideally, your motivation comes from something that aligns well with the company's culture.

What to Avoid:

Some candidates see this as such a broad question that they answer it with personal examples such as "my husband and kids" or "my lake cottage" but the interviewer is typically looking for motivation from a professional perspective.

Example Response:

I am motivated by a team culture that encourages collaboration and innovation. When team members are encouraged to work together to change things for the better, it brings lasting value to the whole organization. There is nothing I like more than envisioning a better way to do something and seeing it come to life.

What do you like to do outside of work?

Question Type:

Background and Personality

Question Analysis:

This may seem like a "softball" question but the interviewer will be paying close attention to your response to see if you are a good fit for the company's culture. Employers look for candidates who make the most of their free time. Your answer should be focused on activities that benefit your own wellbeing and the wellbeing of others in the community.

What to Avoid:

You should avoid discussing activities that sound unprofessional such as "I enjoy drinking and tailgating every Saturday during football season" or "I play video games each night." You should also be careful not to provide a dry response that makes it sound like you have no hobbies. This can create a negative perception about your personality in the eyes of the interviewer.

Example Response:

I am an avid golfer and fly fisherman. I try to play at least one round of golf each week during the spring and summer and I just got back from a fly fishing trip in Yellowstone National Park. I also enjoy giving back to the local community.

What is your management style?

Question Type:

Background and Personality

Question Analysis:

This question is very common when interviewing for management or supervisor positions but may also come up for any role that requires some level of leadership capability. The interviewer wants to know if your management style would be effective for the position and align well with the company's leadership culture. You should focus your response on your leadership traits that would fit well within the company and bring value to the position.

What to Avoid:

You should avoid using absolute words to describe your management style such as "always," "never," or "must." For example, scheduling regular team meetings to encourage team discussion and collaboration is an excellent tactic but if you say, "whenever an issue arises, I always schedule a group meeting to collaborate until we find an answer," it sounds like you react the same way to every problem. You should discuss your style with an emphasis on being able to adapt to a specific situation or to the unique personality traits of your team members.

Example Response:

I believe that the most effective managers are capable of adapting their style to the unique traits of each team member to empower them to reach their full potential. My typical management style is to lead by example, use clear and concise communication, encourage collaboration, and provide constructive feedback. As I get to know my team members, I will often make adjustments to my style to help bring more value to the team. For example, I typically like to meet with each of my team members once per month to discuss their concerns and offer constructive feedback. Last year, I noticed that one of my new team members was second guessing her work which was causing her to fall behind on a project. I decided to adjust my meeting schedule with her to once per week, so I could offer her more regular feedback. I immediately started to see an increase in her confidence which lead to better efficiency in her work. Eventually, she felt comfortable enough to reduce our meeting schedule to once per month. She mentioned that the weekly feedback I offered was a key element in helping her build up her confidence on our team.

Why should we hire you over the other candidates?

Question Type:

Background and Personality

Question Analysis:

This question is almost identical to question #3 but when some candidates are asked to compare themselves to the other candidates, they feel a sense of pressure to oversell themselves to the point of sounding like a used car salesman. However, it is important to remember that you will typically not earn the job offer on a single "grand slam" response. It is earned over the course of a full interview. The interviewer will use this question to learn more about the candidate's strengths and any type of unique value they would bring to the position. You should focus your answer on your strengths that correspond well with the job requirements and try to discuss at least one unique trait that would be attractive to the company.

What to Avoid:

Even though the question invites you to do so, you should avoid making any assumptions about the other candidates such as "I would work harder than any of the other candidates." Negative statements about candidates you likely do not even know can come off as presumptuous and arrogant. Instead, you can acknowledge that you cannot speak for the other candidates, but you feel confident that you are the right fit for the position.

Example Response:

Well, I cannot speak with regard to the other candidates, but I can tell you why I am an excellent fit for the position. My experience leading the development of over 25 successful web applications has put me in a position to understand what it takes to strategize, plan, and execute any type of coding project. My experience leading teams has taught me strong organizational and motivational skills. Aside from my strong skillset that aligns with the position, I am always looking to bring added value to any process or project through innovation. I am never content with a system or process if there is a more effective or efficient way. I typically drive innovation by collaborating with both internal and external resources and by leveraging new technology.

Tell me about a time you set a challenging goal for yourself. How did you ensure that you achieved it?

Question Type:

Behavioral

Question Analysis:

The interviewer will use this question to get a better sense of the candidate's ambition and initiative. They also want to know the strength of the candidate's planning skills when faced with a difficult challenge. In your response, you should focus the discussion around the planning and analysis that enabled you to take calculated actions to achieve your goal.

What to Avoid:

If you have professional experience on your resume, you should typically avoid discussing personal goals such as "I set a goal to lose 50 pounds" or "my goal was to complete a marathon." Instead try to draw on a goal you achieved that relates to your profession. You should also avoid trivial goals such as "I set a goal to arrive at work by 8:30 AM each day."

Example Response:

S: In my previous role as an IT security analyst, I noted that all managers and directors in my department had the Certified Information Systems Security Professional (CISSP) certification in their email signature. I spoke with my manager and learned that the company highly encouraged the certification for IT employees who sought promotions and leadership opportunities.

T: I wanted to place myself in a position to be considered for growth opportunities in our department, so I set a personal goal to pass the CISSP exam within three months. The exam is six hours long and covers eight different subjects, so I knew I would need to create and execute a detailed plan to achieve my goal.

A: Before I started studying for the exam, I reviewed the study materials and spoke with co-workers who had passed the exam to determine the expected number of study hours. I looked through my calendar for the next three months to identify study time outside of the working days and on weekends. After determining that I would need roughly 100 hours to study for the exam, I created a robust plan assigning sections of the preparation materials to each study session on my calendar.

R: It was a strenuous three months, but I remained focused on my end goal to ensure I stayed on task with my study plan. I ended up acing the exam and I accepted a promotion within our department later that year.

Chapter 8: Informational Interviews

Informational interviews are a means to gather information about some specific career field or job. You can conduct these interviews and ask the participants questions before choosing your career.

Advantages of Informational Interviews

Informational interviews are very useful because they help to:

- Narrow down your options

- Prepare you for a specific career

- Discover occupations that you didn't know existed or weren't familiar with

- Gain self confidence and experience when interviewing with professionals

- Discover the types of personalities that thrive in particular career fields

- Have realistic expectations related to employment in particular fields

- Obtain an accurate idea of the existing job market

- Expand your connections with professionals in the field of your choice

How to Start

Choose an Occupation

You should select one or more occupations that you wish to investigate. Decide what information you are interested in acquiring about them. Write down all of the questions you want to get answered.

As with other interviews, it is recommended that you read and gather as much information about the company or organization as you can before you go to the interview.

Identify the People to be Interviewed

You can contact anyone for this type of interview. Start with a list of those people you already know such as your fellow students, friends, neighbors, people who worked with you in the past, or your present coworkers and supervisors. You can visit the alumni office or career center of your college and get the names of those who are currently working in the fields you are interested in. You can approach your family members' acquaintances or public speakers for an interview. Organizational directories, professional organizations, and the yellow pages are some other good resources. Besides this, you can also call a company and ask to speak to someone who has a particular job title.

Conduct Research Before the Interview

In order to conduct an effective informational interview, you cannot go in blindly. It is essential to prepare beforehand. You must do research about various things such as the company, its products, and the person you are going to interview. If you know enough about the company, you will be able to ask in-depth questions related to the job and organization. This in turn will give you the confidence to communicate efficiently.

There are a number of benefits to doing research.

- You can ask more relevant and intelligent questions.

- You can respond more thoughtfully if the interviewee asks any questions.

- You will not waste time by asking questions that can be answered easily by doing some research.

Think about what you want to know about a particular occupation and then figure out the people who may be able to provide that type of information. You can ask the organizations for their pamphlets and brochures to get additional information. The college's library can also be useful for this purpose.

Schedule the Interview

You can contact the person you want to interview in several different ways. You may send a letter or an email, make a phone call, or meet the person personally. You can even ask an acquaintance of the interviewee to get you an appointment.

Letter or Email

You can write an introductory email or letter similar to a cover letter that does not include a job pitch. It can be typed or printed neatly. It must include:

- A short introduction about yourself

- Your purpose for writing to the person

- A brief description of your interest or experience in the individual's field, location, or organization

- Why you wish to talk with the person

- Be straightforward and say you are seeking advice and information

- When and how you will be contacting the person again

Proofread and save the copies of all of the correspondence. Make it a point to contact them again as mentioned. You can call the person on phone and get an appointment. Do not wait for the prospective interviewee to call you on his own. If you are unable to contact the person, you can find out the most suitable time from the receptionist and call again.

Phone or in Person

People who participate in informational interviews usually allot around twenty to thirty minutes to talk about their professional expertise. You should be flexible about scheduling the interview because these interviewees have other commitments. In case a particular volunteer interviewee is too busy, ask him when you can call back and discuss setting up an appointment. Different techniques can be used to request an informational interview. Some good approaches are:

"Hello, I am so and so. I am doing career research related to your occupation. I would like to meet with you and talk to you for around thirty minutes to learn more about this particular job."

"Hi, I am so and so. I am studying at ABC college. I found your name in the organization's directory. I am interested in one day working in a career similar to yours. I hope you can help me to learn more about the job and career options. I would be delighted if you could spare twenty to thirty minutes for an informational interview."

If you want to personally ask the person for an appointment but are unable to meet with him, you can use the receptionists and other support staff as a resource to get information. You can ask them your questions because they may know a lot about the company.

They may be able to tell you how the company works and the job requirements and also name the key people. You should explain to them what you are seeking so that if they feel someone else is better suited to answering questions then, they can refer you to that person. Make it clear that you want to get direct information and will be happy to hear any information they have to share.

Most prospective interviewees are willing to spare twenty to thirty minutes to respond to your question. They may be ready to talk on phone or meet you in their workplace. If you are given a choice between the two, choose to have the interview in the workplace. This will enable you to learn more and make a stronger connection with them.

The Phases

Before the Interview

You should call the person the day before the interview to confirm the appointment. If you are not sure where the interviewee's office is located you can ask at this time. Plan to arrive ten minutes before the interview.

Ninety percent of job openings are not advertised. You may learn about job vacancies that are not found in the newspapers or employment offices through such an interview, so prepare yourself so that you make a great impression. Choose clothing that you would wear for a usual job interview.

During the Interview

Take a pen and notebook: Pretend to be a reporter. It is not necessary to write down everything. However, there might be some phone numbers, names, and other information that you will want to remember.

Take a copy of your resume: Find out what qualities and qualifications the employers look for while hiring. If the situation is appropriate, you can ask the interviewee to review your resume.

Introduce yourself: Once you arrive, you will typically be met by a front desk employee who will introduce you to the interviewee. When you meet him, thank him for taking the time to speak with you. Once again make it clear that you want to learn more about the person's particular career field. Adopt an informal style of conversation during the course of the informational interview.

Be courteous and professional: Maintain good posture and eye contact. Make positive remarks and be light hearted but professional.

Show interest and be enthusiastic: Talk in an informal way and show interest. Ask concise and direct questions. You can refer to the list you have prepared to keep track of your questions but do not curb spontaneous discussion.

Share some things about yourself: You may share some facts related to yourself, but remember that your main purpose is to gather information and learn as much as possible about the field in preparation for a future career.

Many times, the informational interviews turn into employment interviews. If this happens, verify that there is a job opening and emphasize your skills and how they are related to the particular job.

Do not ask for a job: You should not ask for any job during an informational interview. Employers agree to such an interview only because they are sure that it will not be used as an opportunity to seek a job.

If, in the course of the interview, you determine that it is a good job for you, wait until the next day to speak to the employer. The next, call the employer, tell him that the interview helped to confirm your interest in that career, and you wish to formally apply for a position.

The interviewee might offer you a job or an internship. There are many instances where employers have offered jobs to the people who have conducted such interviews. If it is a good offer, go ahead and accept it.

If you ask only for information, you will be treated differently than people who are only interested in a job. Approach the employer by seeking job advice rather than an actual job.

Stay on the right track: Do not waste time asking unnecessary questions.

Listen to them: Listening is a very important part of communication. In addition to asking questions, you should listen carefully. Show them that what they are saying is important to you.

Expand your network of contacts: This interview is like an investment. You spend time with the interviewee sharing information about yourself, asking questions, and getting advice. You are investing your time with him in the hope of gaining something. By spending time with you, he is also hoping to gain something. It is a good idea to keep in touch with each other after the interview ends so that you can both continue to benefit from each other.

Even if the interviewee does not offer you a job, he may be able to refer you to other employers.

Ask for referrals: Before leaving, remember to ask the interviewee if he knows other people who might be willing to speak to you. Ask permission to use his name when contacting potential interviewees.

After the Interview

Thank people: Make sure that you send a letter or card within three days to thank the interviewees. This will help to stay in touch with them. Them that talking to them has been very helpful and that you are grateful to them for taking time out of their day to meet with you. To add a personal touch, you can include a quote they said during the interview. You may also want to ask them to send you any information that they think would be helpful for your career. Include your phone number and address at the end.

Record, analyze, and evaluate: After the interview, remember to write down all of the information that you have gathered. This includes the names of potential future interviewees. Store all of the information together for when you need it. It will be useful for you when you conduct more occupational explorations. Employers are generally impressed by activities like that. It can help pave the way to your ideal job.

When you evaluate the interview, you should ask yourself:

- What is it that you have learned from the interview (consider both the negatives and positives)?

- Does this information that I have gathered match with my interests, values, goals, and abilities?

- What is it that I still have to find out?

- What should my action plan be?

Conclusion

Asking questions can help you to learn about unpublished job opportunities. Even if you do not adopt some formal procedure, just chatting with people on the bus or while waiting in line can lead you to unknown job opportunities.

Questions Asked in Informational Interviews

Here is a list of questions that can be asked during informational interviews:

1. How did you become interested in this particular field?

2. What led you to your current job?

3. How do the knowledge and skills you learned in college apply to this job?

4. Describe your typical day in this job.

5. What future trends do you see for this particular career field?

6. What is your most satisfying accomplishment in this job?

7. <u>What do employers look for in candidates who apply for a job in this field?</u>

8. <u>What is it that you like the most or least about this job?</u>

9. <u>What can I do now to prepare myself for a similar job after I graduate?</u>

10. What advice would you like to give to college students who are interested in this career field?

11. What are the things you learned about this work that you did not know when you graduated?

12. What job search techniques would you suggest for those who have recently graduated?

13. What should I look for in a boss when applying for jobs?

14. What is the "typical" path of this career field?

15. How do employers in this field feel about employees who have a liberal arts degree?

16. Does your organization participate in any internship programs? Can you tell me about them?

17. What are training experiences, trade journals, or professional associations that may help new professionals in this career field?

18. Could I use you as a contact when I start looking for a job or an internship?

Chapter 9: The Power of Storytelling

Storytelling is the ability to tell a story in a way that the listener feels they relate and understand. Anyone can tell a story, but it takes a special type of storytelling for the listener to be able to actually feel what is happening. When you are in a job interview, and the interviewer asks you to tell them about a time something happened, they want you to tell them a story about your past. If your story is uninteresting and not personalized, it is not going to be something that stands out to them. However, if you have a story that they can relate to, and they feel connected to, it could possibly be something that they remember you by and it could even be something that lands you the job.

How can you use this strong tool in your interviews? You can use storytelling when you are answering any long question that requires you to give an example of a time you did something in the past. Examples of these questions are:

- Tell me about a time when you faced a challenge at work, and how you got through it.

- Tell me about a time a decision was made at work and you disagreed with it. How did you handle this situation?
- Tell me your greatest professional strengths and how you have used it in your past employment.
- Tell me about a time when you saw a problem at work and explain how you solved it.
- Tell me about a time when you made a mistake at work and how it was resolved.
- Give me an example of a time when you worked on a team and what helped you accomplish.

These are all questions that are commonly asked in interviews that could benefit from being told an answer in a story format. To do this, you will need some skills in storytelling in the context of an interview. We will look into these skills now.

The first thing that you need to do when telling a story related to an interview question is to remember that the interviewer is looking for the answer. The story can help them to relate to you in a personal way and to see how you have had to deal with struggles in the past, but they want to know the answer to the question. For this, you should always start with the answer. Start with one sentence that completely answers the question. As an example, if you are telling them about a time when you faced a challenge at work and how you got through it, begin by saying that you once had all your staff called in sick on the same day, and you solved the problem by creatively moving staff around in the office to make sure that all of the important tasks got done before the ones that could wait. After you insert with a one-sentence solution, then you can start to tell the details. The details are still helpful, but you want to start with the actual answer so that the interviewer hears it right away and that they know you are responding to exactly what they are asking. Answering the question in the first sentence also shows you are confident in your answer and that you knew what to say right away.

After you answer the question, you can start to provide the background information. The interviewer will likely be interested in this information because they want to know exactly how you accomplished solving your problem. They will want to know all of the details so that they can tell what you are capable of. You can provide the context of why the challenge occurred and why you were the one that had to solve it. Any related information will be interesting and helpful to the interviewer who is listening to your story.

After you provide the context, explain why you were the one that had to deal with the challenge. You'll want to explain your role in the process, talk about how you were the one to solve it, and why it was not the responsibility of everyone else. It can also make you seem like someone who sees problems and fixes them. The way that you word this part of the story is important because it will reflect who you are considered by the interviewer. The interviewer will more than likely love to see you as a leader or someone who sees problems and fixes them. They may not, however, love to see you as the person who made a mistake. For this, it is important how you word this part of the story. You want the story to show all of the good attributes that you have. This is another reason why it is helpful to plan the story out in advance. If you go through the story in advance, you can define your role as something that the employer actually wants to see.

After you define your role, you will want to share the results of the story. This is when you tell how the problem worked out. You can tell if your problem solving worked or if you had to figure out something else afterwards. You do want to keep this step in mind when you are choosing your story that you would like to tell. This is because you want the story to have positive results when you tell it to the person who is interviewing you. You do not want them to see you as a person who failed or someone who does not have the results. Stories of failed results are not stories that should be told in interviews unless they're asked for. For this, you also want to keep this part of the storytelling in mind when you are choosing a story because you want your role to be a positive one. You want your role to portray who you can be, and that is the perfect employee for the opening that the employer currently has.

After you finish telling your story, consider taking some time to make sure that the lesson of your story is clear. You do not want to tell the story in an interview that does not have a purpose or point. You do not want to tell the story that has nothing to do with the question asked. If you think your story only slightly relates to the question, or that its relation was not clear, it is your job to make sure that the lesson of the story is shown clearly by the end of your speech. You can't simply state what the lesson is, or you can use an example to show it to your interviewer. You do not want the interviewer to get the wrong impression; you want them to see the side of you that you were trying to portray. After all, you did just tell an entire story to show why you would be a good fit for a job. Do you want the story to be worth it and come across the way you actually intend?

Let's look at an example. Think about a person who has interviewed you and asked you the question, "Tell me about a time you made a mistake at work, and how you recovered from it." To answer this question in a story format, you could write something like:

"One time, I gave the wrong order to a customer, and I had to fix this problem before the reputation of the business was ruined. When I was 16, I worked in a little old grocery store in the middle of my small town. This grocery store was one of the few establishments in a few miles' radius, so it had multiple different functions. One of the things the grocery store had was a deli counter. Behind the deli counter, was a broiler. This meant that people who came into the grocery store wanted to get fresh broiled chicken. My job, as a teenager, was to cook this chicken.

One day, I got a call that a customer wanted one dozen chicken legs. This was our first order of the day, so I knew we had plenty of chicken. The customer would come in two hours later, so I figured I would just cook the chicken in an hour and a half so it would be hot and ready when they arrived to pick it up. However, when I went over to cook the chicken a half hour before the customer was going to arrive, I found out that there were only 11 chicken legs thawed and ready to cook. This was a big problem. I told the customer that I would have 12 chicken legs ready for them, and I could only have 11. To handle this, I put the 11 chicken legs in the broiler along with a few extra pieces of different parts of the chicken. I then went right to the phone.

Once I got to the phone, I called the customer who ordered the 12 chicken legs. I called them to explain the problem and to offer any solutions that may help. I gave the customer three choices. I told them that they could either wait an extra hour for another chicken leg to unthaw, that they could have a discount on their 11 chicken legs, or that they could have some other pieces of meat along with their chicken legs to make up for the missing piece.

I could have just ignored this and given the customer the eleven chicken legs, hoping that they did not notice that one was missing. This would have been bad customer service, and it would have given the grocery store a bad reputation. It would have affected my job, as I'm sure my boss would have heard of it. It would have affected my guilt level as well because I would have felt bad about not giving the customer what they wanted and what they paid for.

It was not easy to call the customer. It was actually difficult. I had to tell them that I messed up and I did not have what they wanted. However, they appreciated my customer service. They appreciated that I called and told them the truth that I had made a mistake and that I wanted to fix it. They chose one of my three options and happily picked up the chicken. They never complained of the situation, so they must not have been too upset.

The moral of the story is I did not carefully check we had enough chicken before telling the customer that I could give it to them. However, I did help solve the problem in the right way. The story shows me that honesty is always the best policy. Even when I make mistakes, I always need to own up to them to fix them. I learned this at the young age of 16, and I have been perfecting my morals and work ever since."

Looking at this example, it started by telling the answer to the question. It then gave the context and some background information, explained the mistake and finished by sharing the results and making the lesson clear.

Telling stories can be a strong tool in interviews, especially when the interviewer is asking to hear one. Make sure that you have your stories ready in advance so that you can tell the ones that portray your best sides when you are actually in the interview. Make sure to follow the five steps when telling the story so that you can tell it in a way that stands out and shows them everything that you want them to see. If you follow these tips and tricks while telling stories in your interviews, your interviewer will see more into your personality through them, and your stories will show what you are truly capable of. This will make your stories a great addition to your interview skills and help you land your dream job.

Now that we have looked into all of the ways that words and verbal communication can help you and your interviews, let's look into how your nonverbal communication can help you as well.

Chapter 10: Emotional Intelligence in your Job Interview.

First of all, you cannot understand the functioning of the whole world, without understanding yourself. Using emotional intelligence is the first step to be able to look critically at the people around us. Social competences, such as empathy, assertiveness, confidence, cooperation, are essential aspects of your personal life. It depends on it whether we will be the soul of the party, liked, and accepted. We will not achieve this only due to high IQ or scientific knowledge.

It is also worth realizing that during the interview, it is our qualities such as the ability to behave appropriately, the ease of establishing interpersonal relationships, understanding the situation, the skill of persuasion makes up the first impression and can determine whether the employer will see us as a future employee.

Communication Skills at Job Interviews

You have come too far to mess things up. You have done a lot of research, spent your time to gather all that you need for the interview, and even groomed yourself for the occasion. It would be a pity to lose it all for mistakes you did on the actual interview. Remember the objective of your interview is to land a job offer. To realize this objective, you will, by all means, have to prove that you are the best there is. If you are waiting to do big things to blow away your hiring managers, it is time to wake up and smell the coffee. It is the little things that matter and that will possibly work for you or against you.

What to do during the interview

Say Hi to the receptionist

It is common courtesy to greet people you meet. You do not have to start up a conversation, as a matter of fact, it is not recommended that you do. If you can, also get his/her name if it is not on a tag somewhere. This is very important since some hiring managers seek to see just how keen you are and aware of your environment or even friendliness by asking you the name of the receptionist or even the guard at the door.

Which might seem harsh but valid. Hiring managers do not want to hire robots or persons who say they are friendly and do not care enough to know the name of the receptionist or even the guard.

Have the right body language

Your body language will communicate just as much as the information you offer to your hiring managers. You do not want to be in a situation that you say you are confident but your body language reeks of lacking in confidence. Try as much as you can to have your body language convey the same message as your words. If you say you are confident, do maintain an upright posture, maintain eye contact and have a convincing tone.

If slouching, fidgeting and looking down are bad habits that you possess, you can get rid of them by practicing in front of a mirror. Pull up a chair and observe your body language.

Also, avoid flattering behaviors like biting your lower lip or winking. You might be unaware that you wink at people or it is just something you picked up over the years, regardless, you might have to actively subdue them.

Have the right tone of voice

Like your body language, your tone will also speak a thousand words. You could repeat that you know how to do your job a thousand times but if you do not sound like you can, your words are worth nothing. Have a tone that will inspire confidence in your hiring manager.

So, how does one sound more confident during a job interview?

Take your time to think over the question, gather your thoughts before you answer. The recommended time to take for this is five seconds. Now it might seem like such a long time and awkwardness might set in but the interviewer sees it as you giving your answer some consideration.

Always have an interested tone though factual and straight forward. You should keep away from rising your pitch towards the end of your statements as this will turn them into questions making you seem uncertain of what you are saying. You should however vary your tone depending on the question and what it relates to. Do not overdo it though.

Do not apologize for being nervous. Doing this will actually put more scrutiny on just how worried you are about your performance.

Use a firm handshake

There are individuals who are sucker for firm handshakes. There are those who can tell who you are from the way you shake their hand. Just ensure you do not hurt your hiring manager while you are at it.

Sit only when you are asked to

When you walk into the room, only take a seat when they ask you to and not before. It is a sign of politeness. It is the same thing as when someone is at your door. They should wait until you invite them in (especially if you are not as close).

Have your loose items on the floor right next to you

You should never place your items on the interviewer desk unless they say that it is okay that you do so. Have all these items placed comfortably on your lap or on a coffee table right in front of you. As for your briefcase, have it right at your feet or on your side.

Have your mobile turned off

You do not want to have disruptions during the interview. Setting your phone to vibrate just won't cut it.

Thank your interviewer

The fact that they choose you out of the hundreds and thousands of applicants is worth saying thank you.

What not to do during an interview

Do not assume the interview is done until you are out of the door

From the moment you walk in the office the interview is on. Everything from your behavior, use of words to attitude is under scrutiny. As such, you should be overly careful of what you say. After all, everything you say and do will be held and used against you. Be at the very top of our game until you walk out that door, or better yet, out of the company building. You never know who you will bump into on your way out so be respectful to everyone.

Do not be too relaxed

Sure, the interview is a platform for you to gauge is you will love the job and you are encouraged to be relaxed. You should however not treat your hiring manager like your long lost friend (even if he/she is). You should be friendly, but remember you are seeking to be impressive. Being too relaxed may have you slipping up and saying the wrong things altogether.

Never badmouth your old job

Maybe your former boss was the devil incarnate and is probably the reason why you left your previous job. But be it as it may, you should not point it out to your hiring manager. As far as your hiring company is concerned, you should get along with everyone you are given to work with no matter how difficult they are. So rather than badmouth your previous boss or company, speak of the achievements you made as a team. Doing this will also keep you from coming across as self-centered.

Do not freak out if you do not know the answer

Some hiring managers are known for putting their interviewees on the spot. And since you never know what kind of hiring manager you will get, you should always be prepared. Never freak out when you are presented with a question that you do not know the answer to. Freaking out will make you lose all sense of rationality making things even worse. So how should you hand yourself in such a situation?

First, and most important, you should calm down. Freaking out will rise your heart beat rate, rise your temperature and cloud your judgments. Be sure to take deep breaths and convince yourself that all is well. After all, it is okay not to know the answer to a question.

Second, even when you do not know the answer to the question provided, never say that you do not know the answer without giving it a try. Also, as you try to give your answer, do not make things up. Hiring managers are not stupid and will be sure to see right through the crap.

You also have the option of asking follow up questions to ensure you understand the question right. Ask for clarification and more details that will help you provide a better answer.

But even after the clarification, if the question still proves difficult to answer, be sure to iterate what you do know rather than what you do not know. Also, you should spell out the steps that you could take to get to the answer of the question presented. This way, even while you may not have the answer at the moment, you assure the hiring managers that you have the ability to get to the answer if afforded more time.

Never lie

You should, by all means, be straight forward with your hiring manager. It is as they say, the truth always has a way of coming out. When lying, you may not be able to hold a sincere flowing conversation with the hiring manager and this might be a major turn off. Truth be told, honesty is the best policy. Even when you land that job position you will have started on the wrong foot and it is only a matter of time before your lies catch up with you.

Chapter 11: Can You Coach Others?

Interview Question

What have you done to help a peer understand skill areas to strengthen? Give an example.

Why do they ask this question?

Bad Answer

An example of a bad answer to this question would be:

I once had a group member in school who struggled to understand the basic accounting concepts in our accounting class. I knew the person was going to take some time to understand the concepts, so I just ended up doing their work for them so that we could finish the project in a timely manner.

Taking over for the group member helped us get a good grade.

Why this is a bad answer:
Even though you show that your group member has room for development, you don't really show the steps you took to develop them. You don't show that you were interested in developing them. For this question, you

have to show willingness to understand another person's weaknesses, and the desire to help them.

Good Answer

An example of a good answer to this question would be: I once had a classmate in my tax research class ask me how to get better at tax research. I helped them understand what skills and knowledge to strengthen by asking them a series of questions. I asked them if they knew hierarchy of authority in tax research, and I also asked them where they started once they received a research topic. By understanding the person's approach and current knowledge, I was able to develop a plan for them to improve their skills.

Good Answer

An example of a good answer to this question would be: I once had a group member who had a really bad attitude during a group project, so I took the person aside and spoke to them. I told them that they seemed disinterested in the work, and I asked if there was something bothering them.

It turns out that there was something bothering them. They had just failed a project in another class and that is what was affecting them. The group member apologized to me because they weren't aware that they were coming off as disinterested. In this case I was able to provide the feedback in an appropriate manner without embarrassing or offending my group member.

Why this is a good answer:
This is a good answer because it shows how you provided feedback in a tasteful and appropriate manner. You took the person aside and had a personal conversation. You also were not harsh to the person's face.

Interview Question

Give me an example of feedback received and how you put the information to use.

Why do they ask this question?

Are you able to receive feedback without taking it personally?

Can you take feedback and improve on it, or does it go in one ear and out the other?

Bad Answer

An example of a bad answer to this question would be:

One of my prior bosses told me that I was too ambitious and that I didn't need to work so hard. I hear that a lot actually --- that I work too hard.

Why this is a bad answer:

Don't say this in an interview. This is a very typical answer. Nobody like someone that tries to show off by saying that their biggest weakness is working too hard. Just think of a couple of examples where you've received constructive feedback and use those. Do not say your one weakness is that you work too hard or care too much though.

Good Answer

An example of a good answer to this question would be: After a project in school that involved public speaking, I received some feedback from the professor that I was monotoned and slumped over. It was hard for me to take the feedback at first, but I knew that improving my public speaking is key to my success in business. I took the professor's advice, and I also started attending toastmasters to improve my public speaking. After taking the feedback and analyzing it, I performed very well on my next public speaking project I had in school.

Why this is a good answer:

This is a good answer because it highlights not only your ability to take feedback but to also improve on that feedback. This candidate not only received the feedback from the professor, but they also improved their performance in the future by taking the professors feedback positively.

Chapter 12: Master Your Phone Interview

Being interviewed over the phone is a unique and challenging experience. In a limited amount of time, you have to be prepared to sell your appropriateness for the opportunity in order to secure a spot in the next round of interviews. In order to succeed, you will need to understand the different types of phone interviews you may encounter, how to respond most appropriately to the questions asked and what to do in order to gain clarity for the next steps in the process.

So, what is a phone interview? Of course, it is an interview that takes place over the phone but there are a few permutations of the phone interview to prepare for. Sometimes, you may not even realize that you are being interviewed.

The role of the person on the phone is often that of recruiter. The first type of phone interview is not really an interview at all: a recruiter contacting you with the intention of setting up an-in person interview. The recruiter would like to confirm your interest in the position and provide you with the details of when your interview will take place and who you will be meeting with. The recruiter has every intention of setting up an interview for you at this point unless you give her a reason to be concerned.

There could be variety of reasons that the phone call is eliciting concern on the recruiter's behalf such as:

- You answered the call in an unprofessional manner and seem confused as to why you are receiving a phone call. You may not be expecting a call and you are treating the recruiter like a telemarketer until you figure out what the call is concerning.

- You seem uninterested in interviewing for the position.

- You are asking several basic questions about the job, demonstrating that you do not remember much of anything about the company or the role.

- You do not sound professional on the phone. Perhaps you are too focused on the salary or the hours for the position or you are being too candid or lax in your language.

- You cannot be heard or understood. You may be in an area with bad cell phone reception or trying to whisper at your current place or employment or your kids are trying to talk over you when you are on the phone.

As a recent college graduate several years ago, I attempted to answer a call in Times Square from a recruiter representing a large media company. Needless to say, one of the busiest places in the world was (and is) one of the loudest as well. After a few responses of "Can you repeat that?" the opportunity was lost. I was told by the recruiter that he would call me back but that never happened.

- You are inflexible in your availability to come in for an interview. The recruiter may have proposed several times for you to attend an in-person interview but none of those times work for you due to your work schedule or other commitments.

While the recruiter may have called you with every intention of setting up an interview, a point or two of concern may have eliminated your chances. You will be told that you will be contacted once the company has made a decision rather than being called in for an interview.

In some cases, the recruiter attempted to reach you but was unsuccessful in doing so or experienced an area of concern that eliminated that possibility. That may include:

- An unprofessional voicemail message. Your first verbal impression might be your voicemail message so make sure that it is professionally appropriate. Provide a message that clearly states your name that you are sorry that you missed the call and that you will return the call as soon as time allows. Avoid any voicemails messages that include extended words of inspiration, attempts at demonstrating your vocal or rap talents or allowing your kids to record a cute message on your behalf.

- A voicemail message that is not in English or you do not state your name. The recruiter has to know that she reached you. Always provide your name in your message and if you expect that many of the callers to your phone are non-English speakers, provide at least a message in your language of preference as well as one in English.

- Your phone is out of order. Whether it is a permanent change in number or you have used up your prepaid minutes, an out of service phone will lead to a missed opportunity. Unless you possess unique skills that are unlikely to be found in other candidates (and even then), a recruiter is not going to chase you down to find you on social media or email.

- Someone answering the phone who does not take a message for you with all of the necessary details.

So, how can you ensure a smooth phone screening and no stumbling blocks to the in-person interview?

- If you do not recognize the phone number, assume that it may be a recruiter. Answer the call with your name and in a professional manner.

- Be prepared to talk when you answer the phone. If you are unprepared to talk, let the phone go to voicemail.

- If you are prepared to talk but you see that your cell phone reception is very weak or your train is about to go underground, let the call go to voicemail.

- If you planned to be able to talk but something came up unexpectedly, take the recruiter's name and number, and ask when you may call back.

- When you are job seeking, you should have a general idea of your schedule of availability so that setting up an in-person interview is not an arduous process.

- It would be difficult to access every application you have made over the last few months in order to be prepared every time the phone rings but it would be helpful to maintain a basic list that you can quickly peruse for information to refresh your memory once you are contacted.

- If you absolutely have to, fake it until you make it. Make it clear that you are interested in the opportunity when speaking on the phone until you have a reason not to be interested. Do your best to show enthusiasm while you are trying to figure things out.

By following the suggestions above, you will be able to avoid the pitfalls of the seemingly "simple" process of setting up the interview when the recruiter calls you.

All conditions being perfect, it is best to answer the call then and there but sometimes it is not the ideal time. It may be difficult to reach the recruiter later but it is better than to pick up the phone in a bad reception zone or a noisy area.

The next style of phone interview is a pre-screening, which involves being asked a handful of questions to determine if you match the basic criteria needed for the role. The recruiter is trying to avoid having to meet in-person with candidates who are clearly not a fit for the job.

One of the challenges of this type of phone interview is that you may or may not be given a warning in advance. Some recruiters may email you to set up a time for a brief phone screening whereas others will just launch into their questions. What this means is that you must always be prepared. These brief few minutes are your opportunity to sell yourself for the role. The recruiter will not give much consideration to whatever was going on at the time of the call that may have been a distraction to you or hurt your chances of putting your best foot forward.

While you cannot anticipate all of the questions that may be asked, the questions do tend to veer to the basics during a phone screen. A recruiter will generally not have an expert knowledge of the position that you are interviewing for. He will be looking for a basic skills match and looking to weed out people with major question marks in their backgrounds.

The key here is that time is limited. The recruiter is trying to determine your basic fit for the role. Similar questions may be asked by the same person during an in person interview, which you can answer with greater depth and detail at that time.

No matter what questions are asked, consider the following:

How can I demonstrate that I am a great fit for this role when I answer this question? An interview isn't about you but an opportunity to show why you are a great fit for the job.

Without having the opportunity to see someone in person, there is a connection that is lost over the phone.

Try to project a good level of energy and enthusiasm over the phone. If normally you are subdued and a quiet talker, you may need to push yourself outside of your comfort zone for the phone interview. In order to project your voice and maintain your enthusiasm, you may want to stand up for the phone interview and speak a bit louder than you normally would. Although it might be tempting, avoid pacing around. Your phone might hit certain bad reception areas if you are walking around so avoid having the phone cut in and out.

If you are given the opportunity to prepare for the phone screening, there are several steps that you can take to put your best foot forward:

Research: When you know that you have a phone screening to prepare for, don't be reliant upon remembering what you learned about the company when you submitted your resume. Look up the company website and read current articles about the organization.

Review: Reread the job description for the position (you saved it, right? If not, a Google search might help you to find the old posting), the cover letter that you sent as well as your resume.

Consider: What questions you might be asked about your background and determine how you can explain any bumps in your career journey- such as an inconsistent work history or if you have ever been fired.

If you need to, admit to any mistakes or errors in judgment but focus on what you have learned as well. Try to stay light on the negativity and focus on the positive.

Space: Find a quiet area where you will be taking the call. If you are at home, make sure that your family knows that you have an important call at that time and you will let them know when you are off of the phone.

Do not ask about the salary over the phone. Just like it is not appropriate to ask about the salary during your first in person interview, it is not appropriate to ask here either.

The recruiter might ask what salary you are seeking as a way to weed out candidates over the phone. Provide a wide salary range as opposed to a number. Once you have responded, you can inquire as to what range the company has in mind.

When you are asked if you have any questions, don't focus on the hours of the job or the fringe benefits. Use this as your opportunity to gain clarity on the next steps in the process as well as the recruiter's contact information.

Ask what are the next steps in the process and when you can expect to hear back. This will provide you with a timeline for your follow up strategy. If you are told that you will hear back within two weeks, it would be acceptable for you to contact the recruiter again somewhere in the range of two and a half to three weeks later.

Make sure to get the recruiter's full name and email address. Email the recruiter a thank you note within one day of your phone interview. Avoid a generic note that can be used for anyone at any time. Include a couple of specific details that were discussed and a reference as to your strong qualifications.

"Dear Ms. Thomas,

Thank you for taking the time over the phone to discuss the position of Systems Analyst. I enjoyed learning more about the organization's planned expansion into the South American market. Given my knowledge of the region and relevant experience in the areas of banking and finance, I am excited to learn more. I am looking forward to the next steps in the process.

Regards"

The third, and final, type of phone interview is not a pre-screening but your actual "first interview". The most common reason that the first interview takes place over the phone is for logistical purposes: candidates from outside of the geographic area are being considered for the position and to be respectful of everyone's time, the phone interview is replacing the need to travel to an in-person interview. This style of interview is becoming less commonplace as interviews with remote candidates are more commonly being conducted over Skype or similar web based application.

Being able to participate in a formal interview over the phone does have some advantages for the applicant. As you cannot be seen by the interviewer, you can keep your notes in front of you. This might include a list of the questions that you want to ask, reminders of particular accomplishments that you want to be sure to mention and possibly even your resume.

If there is more than one person on the other end of the line, you have to pay special attention as to when it is your time to talk. The first interviewer may have just finished talking and you are ready to respond but the second interviewer has something to say. When there is more than one interviewer, allow a brief moment before you respond to each question before you respond.

As opposed to a briefer pre-screening interview, you should provide answers that go more in-depth and paint a picture of your strong qualifications for the job.

Chapter 13: Reviewing The Interview

You've articulated your strengths, you've learned to tell your story, and you've practiced to become your very best. Now what?

Even though you've gotten much better at interviewing by learning how to communicate your story, you probably won't deliver a knockout performance in every interview. The truth is that there is always room to get better, and there is one thing in particular you can do to get even better at interviewing. Evaluate how the interview went and think about your perceptions of the organization *before* they give you a job offer.

Why bother thinking about something that just happened?

People have a tendency to believe that any given outcome was inevitable once it has happened, even if they didn't know what the outcome would be before it happened. If you wait until you hear that an organization is not interested in hiring you, you may think that you knew this was going to happen all along. When you think back on the interview after having been turned down, it will inevitably seem like it went poorly. You may blame yourself, the interviewer (perhaps they didn't ask you the right questions), or someone else (perhaps there are many overqualified job seekers in your area, and they're taking all the entry-level jobs that should be given to younger people). Your memories will have faded and you'll think back on only the negative aspects of the interview.

Alternatively, what if you're offered the job? It's tempting to believe that this means that your interviewing skills are absolutely amazing and you couldn't have done any better. You might feel that you don't even need to practice the next time you decide to look for a job. After all, you're a master, and getting future jobs will be as easy as showing up to interview on the scheduled day. (We hope you can read our sarcasm.)

Putting an interview experience out of mind as soon as you walk out the door can also lead you to make the wrong decision about accepting the job. If you're presented with a strong job offer, you may find yourself deciding that you really like the organization. Perhaps the hiring manager said a lot of great things about you when they called with the offer; maybe they talked up all of the benefits you would receive if you worked there.

If you have received an offer without already deciding whether the organization is right for you, it will be really difficult to objectively evaluate their offer. That decision is too important to let someone make for you.

And if you're still not convinced that you need to reflect on your job interview, do it for another reason. If nothing else, writing down the questions that you answered well, or the questions that you didn't address particularly well, gives you great content for a thank you letter.

For all of these reasons, it's best to evaluate the interview experience before you learn its outcome. It is very important to *write down* your perceptions so you don't forget them later. With written notes, you'll have an objective impression of how the interview went that you can then use to improve your interview skills in the future as well as to decide whether you want to accept a job offer.

How to Reflect on Your Interview Experience

As soon as you have a moment to yourself after the interview is over, think about your overall impressions.

Then think about the interview in chronological order, stopping at each memorable event (walking into the office, shaking hands, greeting your interviewer, and so forth) and again at each interview question that you can remember. Evaluate each of these in your mind and then compose written notes.

After thinking about the interview by yourself, talk about the experience with several people. Ideally, these should be people who will ask you a lot of questions. Conversation will help you to reflect on things that may have escaped your attention. For instance, a friend might ask if people were smiling in the office. If you talk about this on the same day that you had the interview, you'll be able to remember whether you saw people who seemed to be happy to be at their jobs. If you try to remember this next month when you're evaluating the job offer, your recollection won't be as accurate.

Next, jot down what you learned about the company. What are the expectations that were communicated to you? What did you learn about the company culture? Were they asking questions that focused on specific tasks or skills? If so, these will probably be key to your success on the job.

Finally, think through the highlights, lowlights, and what you plan to do in future interviews. To help you along in this process of evaluating your interview, we've created an Interview Evaluation Guide.

Interview Evaluation Guide

Overview

- How well prepared did you feel walking into the interview?
- <u>Which questions surprised you or caught you off guard?</u>

The positives

- Which of your answers best communicated your story? What worked about those answers?

The negatives

- Which of your answers did not communicate your story very well? Why did they fall short? (Perhaps your answer didn't fit with the rest of your story or was confusing. Maybe you just couldn't think of an answer.)

The company

- Did you get a clear sense of what you would do on a daily basis?

- Do you know who you would work with? Who would you report to? Who would you interact with on a daily basis? Who would you interact with only occasionally?

- Do you think you could get along reasonably well with the people you met? (Include everyone you interacted with, not just the interviewers.)

- Do you think this position will allow you to use your skills and knowledge and help you meet your career goals?

- Do you know what will be expected of you, how you will be evaluated, and what you will need to do to excel in this position?

- <u>Are you excited about the possibility of working for this organization and with these people?</u>

For the future

- What might you do differently during your next interview?

Disliking an organization

If you don't like to fail, you may find yourself writing something like, "I don't think I liked this organization." That way, you'll be able to soothe your ego if they don't extend you an offer. You'll just say to yourself, *that job would have been awful—I'm glad they didn't bother calling me back!*

It's fine to write down negative opinions if they are in fact true. But try to avoid being pre-emptively negative in order to save your feelings. This is a little like breaking up with someone just so they don't break up with you first. Why not give it a little time? It's okay to like a job or an organization even if you're not exactly the right fit, right now. That doesn't mean you'll never get to work there. In fact, a better position may open up in the future, or your future work experiences may make you a more desirable candidate.

If you evaluate an organization negatively just to feel better about rejection in the future, you'll also be less likely to be happy or satisfied with the job offer when it does come. You'll look back at your written reflections and think, *oh, but I didn't like this organization. Maybe I shouldn't accept the offer.*

If you're always evaluating jobs or organizations negatively and you know that it's not because you're afraid of rejection, you may be applying to the wrong jobs. In this case, it's time to do more research about organizations before you bother applying and going on interviews and to honestly evaluate whether this is indeed the field you want to work in. For instance, if you find yourself frustrated that every banking job in New York City requires ridiculous hours, perhaps you need to consider living in a different area or working for a less prestigious firm where the expectations may be a little lower.

Success is Not Measured in Job Offers

You should always remember that whether or not you get a job offer shouldn't define how well the interview went. You can make a great impression in the mind of an interviewer and still not be the best fit for the job. If you are considering a job offer and reflecting on the interview, keep in mind that the cost of a bad fit is high for both you and your employer. If you don't think you can deliver what the job requires, it may be best for you to pass on the offer. And instead of thinking about whether you aced an interview, instead of letting the outcome dictate how you feel about the process, you can define for yourself whether or not the interview was a success. If you can remember this while you're in the interview itself, it will help you be more objective and less nervous. It will also help you to stay positive throughout the whole job search process.

Chapter 14: Dealing with Realities

A well thought out job search that focuses on the right fit starts with some definitions.

- What industry or industry segments do you want to work in?
- Do you want to work in an established company or one new to the industry?
- Where would you most like to work or where else would you be willing to accept a relevant job geographically?
- Given your present circumstances, how much of a risk-taker are you?

Clearly, your perception of yourself, and how you are convinced that others see you, helps you rebrand yourself. Positive results that are relevant to the needs of your target company, and presented credibly, are what will get you in the door and give you the opportunity to excel. But to get there, you have to deal with realities: besides company financial status, try to measure the quality and staying power of the management.

You should understand the status of products and services, morale factors affecting productivity or turnover, and the gaps and pains the company needs to resolve to improve its competitiveness and profitability. The level of your success depends heavily on how well your experience and results can help close the gaps and manage the pain.

Before you get too far into your decision making, make sure to check your priorities and share your thoughts with the people who most matter in your life.

Where do you start?

Unless you're single and responsible only for yourself, your first reality check is your family. If you're married, start obviously with your spouse. Hopefully, there are no surprises. If you've been out of work, your spouse is well aware that you need to produce income and also well aware of what kind of situation can restore your confidence, make you happiest and probably most successful.

If an important new job requires a move, then what? One of your many considerations may be spouse employment.

Do you go alone for a while until you're sure things will work the way you envisioned while your spouse continues to work and maybe starts his/her own job search? What about children? Do you have kids in school? If they're very young, they're probably also very malleable. They can move and make new friends in days and this can turn out to be wonderful adventure for them. If they're older, not so easy. It depends on what grades they're in school, what outside activities and, maybe more than anything else, what close friendships they may have to leave behind.

The importance of family support

Your family is your main source of support. If you really like the new opportunity, you may need to sell a lot to get them onboard. Selling in this case is to illustrate benefits to them, dealing first with emotions like fear, anger and insecurity, especially over losing friends and facing the changes inherent in a strange new place. While they may resist and experience some temporary setback, you need to first overcome the emotions and then convince them that this new situation is good for them. Not an easy task. But an extension of your role as a salesman.

If you force them to go literally kicking and screaming, or with arms folded across their chests, and given to spurts of anger or crying jags, can you possibly focus enough on your new job to make positive impressions? Maybe you can clear your head and focus during the day, but what about coming home? How much resistance can you put up with and for how long?

Add to that the possibility of leaving behind, or taking with you, elderly or sick parents and the various complications you can imagine.

None of this is meant to scare you or turn you off to what you think could be a great opportunity. It is meant to condition you to the realities, including all of the circumstances you need to be aware of in this life-changing decision.

You want a job with growth potential, where you can excel and maximize your income. Getting to that point is not as simple as finding an ad and acing an interview. It is hard work. Maybe even tedious work. And it takes thoughtful, disciplined research. You never want to make a decision, particularly if it involves a move that can blow up in your face because of factors you didn't know, and, therefore, didn't anticipate. What do you do then? Go back into a job search and possibly move again after your family has gotten settled?

Even if you are fortunate enough to find an opportunity that does not require a move, is it possibly a temporary relief from a problem that could wind up being worse sometime down the line. Make sure to uncover both the good and the bad of the company and its management. Whatever you decide, keeping up the confidence, respect, security and support of your family is fundamental to your success.

Never give up on research

If you can read between the lines and understand where I am going with this, your smartest approach is to invest as much time and effort as possible into meaningful research. And, if you can, find ways for your family to help you. You may be surprised by ideas they come up with and people they may know who can be valuable sources of information. You want to do this right.

Find that situation that lets you excel, where your family, each member, sees something positive. For your spouse, maybe a better job as well, or a better house, better neighborhood, better activities or social circles. For the kids, maybe better schools or camps or colleges than you couldn't have afforded before, along with greater, affordable social opportunities. Maybe a car. You get the picture.

If they are all happy, it is much easier for you to approach that new job with a vigor and excitement that wins you recognition. And it is much easier to come home at night to smiling faces eager to tell you about their new experiences.

My appreciation, and love, of research was instilled in me early in my career by some of the toughest critics I could possibly imagine. They shaped my thinking in ways that have served me well throughout my career. I am grateful to them for whatever successes I have had. And, in retrospect, I've thought many times how glad I am that I was receptive and eager to learn from them. I hope in this book, and particularly in this chapter, that I can pass on some of their wisdom.

As a young journalism student, I had the good fortune of learning from seasoned, street smart newspaper editors who were not impressed by academic writings, but insisted on "clear, correct and concise" articles on any subject. Those words became a mantra. They insisted on the use of correct words, corroboration of facts and background for stories along with absolute adherence to deadlines. I think back sometimes to what I thought were excellent pieces of copy that wound up being slashed and marked up beyond belief. And sometimes even ridiculed.

I once used the word "penultimate" in writing about a tennis player advancing to the semi-finals of a tournament. The loud "you got to be kidding me" response from my instructor obviously has stuck with me as a reminder to express, not impress, with my writing.

An editing assignment a little later on in which a New York Times writer referred to a car "careering" over a curb and into a wall served as another long-time lesson. I confidently changed the word to "careening."

The instructor, who, at night was the editor of The New York Times foreign desk, called me out in class and asked me what "careening" meant and I confidently answered him (to sway to the side). Then he asked me what "careering" meant and I made an attempt to answer, defending my change and learning a lesson in research when the editor asked me publicly if I had bothered to look up the word or had just chosen to assume I knew more than the writer.

I had mistakenly changed the writer's meaning and imagery. Careering, I learned, meant plunging straight ahead, not swaying to the side. My argument that the word "careering" didn't fit the "clear" part of the mantra fell flat and I learned quickly to make frequent use of both a dictionary and a thesaurus.

A few years later, Journalism degree in my pocket and a graduate of a Defense Department training program, I was an intelligence analyst at the National Security Agency, where research is a challenging and demanding full time business. I collected and analyzed data on a variety of targets, then had to learn to write reports using only precise adjectives and strictly supportable facts. Adjectives like "long" or "short," "big" or "small" or colors like "red" or "blue" or "green" can be interpreted in so many different ways by different people as to be generally meaningless and unsupportable.

The rule of thumb was that each fact had to be proven with input from five different sources and, where possible, was appended with statistical research and photographs. The work was painstaking and exacting, but the sensation of having reports accepted for distribution was exhilarating. With all the bad raps NSA has taken in the past few years, I learned to respect the dedicated professionalism that went into intelligence products. I am still influenced by what I learned there many years ago.

You'll probably never have to write with only absolutely precise adjectives and prove everything you say from five sources, but you will need to learn the discipline of looking at facts through clear eyes, without prejudgment. That will help you analyze and assess industries, companies and people who may influence the rest of your life.

Getting into your "best" company

So, you've identified the industries, the companies and the people you want to pursue. Now what? You want to capitalize on all of the effort you've put into finding industries where you would have the most comfort and expertise and then companies within those industries where the past results of your skills and experience could be most valuable.

Using any sources, including the internet, see if you can find speeches or articles by key executives to get insights into what is going on right now or in the immediate future. With luck, you might find something from an executive in your area of specialization that could be extremely useful in both gaining entry to the company and in interviews.

Don't hesitate to write to someone whose article or speech has impressed you. Look also at press releases to get a better sense of how the company wants to be perceived by its various publics, especially shareholders and customers.

Sift through your notes and drop companies that give you concern. Consider what you're doing as a step towards a long-term relationship. Are you willing to commit long hours, enthusiasm and passion to this organization which may, in fact, consume most of your daily thoughts, not to mention time? Maybe even more than your home life. Are the potential rewards worth the potential risk? As much as possible, make up your mind objectively, with research as your basis.

Don't be talked into a job where there are serious questions. That said, no company, and no job, is perfect. There will always be some level of anxiety. Go back to the earlier thoughts about knowing yourself and make a reasoned decision based on the best intelligence you have been able to muster. Imperfections in a company may be opportunities for you depending on your experience and ability to fix them.

By now, you should have a short list. Maybe even a single company. But, remember, there are no sure things. Hedge a bit. Have alternatives. A Plan "B". Maybe more.

In preparation for your approach to a company, find out what you can about the executives, particularly those who conceivably could influence your future. How old are they? How long have they been with the company? How successful have they been here and in previous organizations? Did they by chance go to the same school or schools that you did? What outside organizations are they involved with?

Most importantly, is there anything in their backgrounds that ties to you? Or to someone you know well? That also could aid your entry into the company. Your very valuable business librarian should be able to steer you to biographical references, by name or by company.

If you can find, or get introduced to, current or former employees of your target companies, ask about these executives. What do these people know or hear about them? Do they have a reputation for fairness and a history of supporting and developing subordinates? Ask their impressions of the company and, while you're at it, check out Glassdoor and similar websites that can provide insights into the company. If you don't know people personally, one of the best ways to find them is through LinkedIn.

Keep moving forward

As in intelligence work, you'll rarely find everything you would like to know. But the more you do find that objectively satisfies your interest, the more your enthusiasm should be piqued. And, presumably, you can find valuable information that can get you in the door and be knowledgeably impressive in interviews. The quality and usefulness of your research should allow you to separate yourself from your competition and give you an opening to prove your worth.

You are now ready to move into the next phase of your strategy: Getting in the door. You might get lucky through your research and establish contact with a key executive, in person, at a business meeting or by phone or letter, or through networking. If you got that person's attention, most likely he/she would contact HR and have them interview you. That's a plus because it moves you to a short list (maybe the top) and requires that the HR people report the results of the meeting to the key executive.

Remember, the comment earlier about being the CEO of You? Well, now you're in charge. Excel in the interview and your chances of landing the job have just soared.

The most likely scenario is that you will need to network into a position which, because of an implied endorsement, may be more powerful than the direct contact. It involves an extra step or two but helps you build relationships for now and the future.

Especially after you have the advantage of learning how to effectively use principles and strategies of networking.

Conclusion

In summary, a job interview is one of the most important meetings in the working life of a person. Interviews serve as a good chance for the employer to assess a prospective new team member, while the candidate assesses their potential bosses. Interview preparation offers candidates the necessary tactics on how to conduct themselves to increase their chances of having a successful interview. Conversely, lack of preparation leads to nervousness and mistakes during the interview process.

As a basic guideline, this book equips a job candidate, whether starting up or experienced candidates, with necessary techniques to ace their next interview process. It offers a step-by-step guide on things one needs to know and do before an interview, things to do during the interview, and things one needs to know and do after the interview. It portrays the significance of reading prior to an interview since it shows candidates how to market themselves to the prospective employers and to be able to assess if the job offer is suitable for them in the process. It also offers insight into the things that should be avoided during an interview. If this guideline is followed, a candidate is assured of ultimate success in their next interview.

www.ingramcontent.com/pod-product-compliance
Lightning Source LLC
Chambersburg PA
CBHW070342220526
45467CB00001B/223